The Experience
of Praying

SEAN CAULFIELD, O.C.S.O.

PAULIST PRESS
New York/Ramsey

Library of Congress
Catalog Card Number: 79-92428

ISBN: 0-8091-2358-4

Published by Paulist Press
Editorial Office: 1865 Broadway, New York, N.Y. 10023
Business Office: 545 Island Road, Ramsey, N.J. 07446

Printed and bound in the
United States of America

THE EXPERIENCE OF PRAYING

Contents

Introduction

Contemplatives are everywhere. They are the people who gaze and wonder, the searchers after the hidden meaning of things. They are not driven by achievement or status. This makes their prayer and behavior strange and unconventional at times. What drives them is a hunger for fulfillment, a hunger for others and for an Absolute. They are satisfied only with the possession of a total good.

This book is more about the experience of praying than about the science of prayer. It tries to take a look inside the mind of the person at prayer, his attitudes and values. The experience of praying is not an exercise that bypasses life. It is a hunger and a search for the God of events and acts who involves himself in the ups and downs of our daily history. Praying interprets life by reflecting on it in the context of God. For that reason this is not only a book of ideas and insights but also of memories and events that are inseparable from my own experience of praying.

It has never been the intended purpose of contemplative praying that one should arrive at some mystical experience of an extraordinary nature. That this might happen is beside the point. The purpose of prayer is that one should, in Christ, arrive at a surrender in love to the Father. In Christ's Spirit this is possible. It is not the abandonment of one's personhood but the discovery of one's essential freedom.

Contemplative praying is no tranquilizer. It touches every aspect of life, revealing who we are to ourselves and to God. It integrates our powers—enabling us to accept ourselves as we are with all our human incompleteness. It enables us to love ourselves because it reveals how deeply we are loved by God. It is a preservative in our life. We are gradually set free from the grosser aspects of sin: pride, fanaticism, hardness of heart, harshness toward others, compulsions to control.

There are no special exercises in self-discipline required for progress in praying other than fidelity to the truth about ourselves. It is this fidelity that tears away the false mask. It cleanses the eye of the mind, making an empathetic awareness of God and others possible. If creative insights are needed they will be received when necessary. They cannot be conjured up through mere desire.

These pages tell of the search through nothingness and incomprehension for the wholly other God. They tell of the pain and the joy in praying, and in discovering within it the meaning of life. They suggest that what was experienced by the mystics of an earlier age is available to all of us. There is a difference, of course, but it is only in our degree of participation. The mystics did not compromise. We do. We also fail to reflect from a faith stance on the deeper meaning of what is happening to us.

The first chapters deal with apophatic prayer—the prayer of faith; the struggle with darkness, nothingness and suffering; the search for God in an apparently meaningless inner life. The middle portion of the book deals with praying as it affects and interprets our activity—our life-style as incarnational presence of God. The final chapters deal with cataphatic prayer—the light coming through; the awareness of transcendence; the grace and friendship of God in a prayer beyond words or concepts. The autobiographical passages serve merely to illustrate the growing understanding of God. These three aspects of prayer are not rigidly separated into three distinct sections in the book for the simple reason that in real life they constantly intermingle.

At the end of each chapter there is a "What to do" section. These short sections have to do with technique and structure. They are not intended to be the content of one's prayer but simple introductions that might enable a person to quiet down and focus attention. Prayer itself must be allowed to develop freely. We must discover the way of praying that suits ourselves, celebrating its purifying aspects without self-pity and its joys without egotism.

1. No-Thingness

I've come at last to know that God is not a "thing." He is not of the things and bits of his own creation, one more objective thing "out there," something amongst other things. He is not even the supreme thing, the first or best or greatest in a series. He is not relative to anything. He is the altogether Other, the Mystery that cannot be contained or boxed in by any symbol or concept. Our response is awe, not understanding. If we find ourselves involved in a personal way with him the experience may well be one of being invaded with a sense of "no-thingness." All our self-protecting strengths and securities are swept from under our feet.

The sense of nothingness is painful. Back in the days when I struggled with the Other, the mystery and no-thingness of God, all I had to live with was a sense of despair. Praying is not something one does as a nice clean intellectual exercise at certain fixed times. There are fixed times but prayer is inseparable from what is happening historically in one's life. For myself it was often a prayer of silent longing, a prayer in deeds rather than in words. Something was always happening, changing, becoming and I never knew what it was or why. At least not until later. Changing and becoming is always painful. It was dark in the basement of the abbey church. Down there, beyond the toolroom and the cooler, I had fixed up a place with plasterboards where I could have privacy and silence. I would pray there each morning from 4 A.M. to 6 A.M., wrestling with God, with noth-

3

ingness and meaninglessness. Those feelings were made concrete by the fact that in a Trappist abbey one could look forward ten, twenty or thirty years and be able to tell precisely what on any given day, at any given time, one would be doing. This predictability robbed the future in some fashion or other of meaning. The reaction was a sort of inner despair, a death in the midst of life. It was then I began to look back and see that nothing had happened, and I began to realize that nothing was going to happen. There would be a quiet descent to the grave in diluted mediocrity, and that would end that. I did not realize at the time that the transcendent otherness, the mystery of the no-thingness of God was then and there emerging into my consciousness and into my life. The No-Thing would really happen. This sort of wrestling with God is never simply an emotional or intellectual problem. It is concrete in what is happening in other areas of one's life. The tensions developed in crises of growth in a Trappist abbey are supposedly relieved through manual work. It didn't work out that way for me. Periodically, when it built up to a climax, I would pass out and empty out. Bathrooms were not designed for my versatility. I would sit with a basin on my lap and occasionally return to consciousness cramped between the bowl and the door. It was an outer symbol of inner nothingness. But it brought relief and it had a certain necessity in it.

At that time I could not fit my understanding of God into my scheme of things. It was a mistake, of course, trying to understand the Ineffable and a greater mistake trying to fit him neatly into my narrow life. But in spite of all my pain he did not seem to intervene or care very much about my nothingness. I had yet to learn that sharing our human condition, making of our struggle a divine experience, was a far greater thing than isolated miracles of intervention. At the moment, however, it seemed to me that he was up there with all the answers, like a teacher at the blackboard. Everything was well ordered in a nice clean heaven where everybody observed the ten commandments. And he was waiting in eternal rest, without malice but without noticeable enthusiasm, for all of us to make the right moves. I realized that if we made the wrong moves he would, in his mercy, readjust to our stupidity and we could begin all over again. It was difficult to generate any enthusiasm for such a God. It always is for what has been called the "night of purgation," pure faith, interior asceticism. I used to think that if I knew his will and did it I would have a meaningful life. If I could discover some hidden plan up his sleeve—but there was no such plan. Faith, in light or in darkness, is more than ethical behavior, and the Church more than the custodian of public and private morals. What I was involved in was the beginning of a serious encounter of love with a personal God and it was killing me. But it was also setting me free, free to take responsibility for my life and to make decisions. God would be always with me—the plans were mine to make. That kind of inner freedom comes when we abandon our security and are drowned in his no-thingness. At that price who wants to be free? It is so much easier at that point to quit altogether or just regress to childish faith practices that worked in the past.

Monks are honest, forthright, prayerful people. That sort of honesty is a tremendous challenge and more than a bit exasperating. The unflinchingly sincere have a way of making one feel the burden of one's phoniness. I used to walk down the cloister behind one such person. His monumental buttocks would heave to the right and give a little twitch, then heave to the left and give a little twitch. It was the twitch that was insulting. With my eyes glazed by this phenomenon of nature I was goaded to fury. As a struggling monk would, in those days, I prayed: "Jesus, meek and humble of heart, make my heart like unto thine." It was a focus for my own nothingness. In a Trappist abbey, a so-called "power-house of prayer" whose men were austere to the point of being human works of art, these buttocks had no meaning and my life had no meaning. I was of the opinion that if I stopped being rotten by achieving a holy way of life I would find meaning. But a way of life that could, by reflection, be considered holy would be disastrous. It was the condition of the Pharisee at the front of the Temple who had fulfilled all the ethical requirements but had not learned to love. God alone is holy, and if ever the day comes when we participate in it, it will never be in a way that allows us to gloat in it. One thing was coming clear: any form of monkish posturing or politics added nothing but despair to the search for meaning.

"All" and "nothingness" have something in common. Through the nothingness we come to a sense of the All. Put together all the people and all the bits and pieces of the universe and you will still be asking: "Is this all?" The answer will still be "No." The human heart hungers for the Absolute. It opens out beyond the sum total of things, seeking infinity. "All" may be approached through concentration—focusing one's attention so as to block out the multiplicity of individual things. Or it may be approached through nothingness—the loss, pain, suffering, dread when individual things and people fail us and we fail ourselves. "All" is not one other thing that might fail us, nor any collection of things nor their inner dynamic. It is the transcendent God encountering us, the God who is not a part of things nor yet apart from them.

Nothingness is not nonexistence. It is something positive, the space for being. The nonexistence where a being should be is a possible description of sin. One has to go from sin as nonexistence to nothingness as the space for God, the mysterious ground of existence. It is not something in one's head but a lived-out experience. I came to know what it meant to be a sinner sitting in the dark in the basement. The mask formed by acceptance, status, projects, success was stripped away. I could see my true self as sinner. I could also see that I was not my own savior. There was nothing within my own self that could save me out of my sinfulness. The obvious conclusion to that line of thought, if one were living by reason and logic alone, was to despair. However, the experience was necessary in order to get a grasp on the mystery of hope. It was a time of struggle. I was distracted by many thoughts of suicide. God was "out there" somewhere and didn't seem to care. There were lots of ropes in the toolroom. There would be an element of revenge on life in it also, but I knew in my heart that it would be the cowardly way out and that I would never do it. This was my life. I could face it and survive. It did not even remotely strike me that there might be anything emotionally or mentally wrong with me. I do not think there was. I was learning that individual things controlled and enslaved me, taking away spontaneity. I had to experience nothingness if All were to be found. We do not remain attached to what hurts us. It is not such a bad thing that we sometimes hurt ourselves. If we let it be we become more free and tolerant. Then everything comes back again but without the control.

If there was a solution to my sinfulness and despair it had to come from someone other than myself, from someone greater who could reach in with power and save me. By saving me I meant giving me a reason for being. I needed God, not a powerful God outside me who might impose some sort of salvation on me out of pity. If he did not involve me in the process, merely giving me a handout, I would still remain an isolated meaningless and useless self. Nor would it be sufficient if he did it along with me in a sort of parallel action, he doing his part and I doing mine. To be really saved from the despair and meaninglessness of life he would have to be within me, within every inadequate thought and decision and act. He would have to be so intimately present that he transformed me from within, so present within my acts that while remaining hopelessly inadequate they became adequate. That is hope. It has nothing to do with expectations.

Expectations are seldom fulfilled. Living on expectations is too easy. It is a way of refusing to grapple with the present as meaningful. I had lived for years on expectations. Something would happen. Life would be changed. Now I was beginning to realize that hope was something happening in the "here and now." Living one's life on daydreams is a waste of time. Hope is the child of mercy and despair—God's mercy and our despair. It is nourished on the death of expectations. It was peaceful to let expectations die, to accept the rich no-thingness of God—his utter mystery, his transcendent awesomeness that cannot be grasped or controlled; peaceful to learn to live with human incompleteness, with the reality of the human inglorious condition, with the awareness now of God's presence within the incompleteness, within the failing effort. Our failure, like the failure of Christ in death, is the very revelation of God as present and saving and loving. His withinness makes the incomplete complete, the failing effort adequate. Salvation is a gift to be received, not a task to be done. There are no self-made men and women in prayerful living. The self-made people are trapped in status, politics and empty ritual.

It is essential then to realize that the nothingness, meaninglessness and seeming despair are an integral part of contemplative praying. They are our first reaction to the dark experience of the inrush of God whose inner essence is not of our creation and cannot be expressed in terms of that created world. His essence is unselfish love and it calls and uproots us. When we take him seriously he does not connive with our self-centered pettiness.

What to do

Sit with God as you might with the ocean.
You bring nothing to the ocean, yet it changes you.
Or sit with God as you might with your health.

If you are healthy you receive no special messages
from your internal organs . . . there is simply
a harmony of togetherness.
Let go of all and go out to All.
Let the Mystery empty you from within.
Surrender your life in faith to his silent presence.
Be silent.

2. Given-Awayness

Love is sacrificial. The lover is given-away. The love is in the vulnerability, the availability, having nothing you are unwilling to part with but everything offered and given to the one loved.

There are people who love with a great degree of heroism. I have known some. For most of us however there is a point at which we arrive rather quickly beyond which we are unwilling to move. We say, or imply: "This is all I can give . . . ask no more . . . you are asking too much of me."

I remember when I was a seminarian in Ireland, long before I joined the Trappists. I was very vain about my black suit, white shirt and black tie—how ludicrous are the clerical colors that give us status and rank. A poor man came begging to the door. He was a young man in his late twenties or early thirties. He had a wife and one child, and they lived in a small canvas tent, traveling from place to place in Ireland's wet and cold. I gave him some money, a half-crown. Relative to what I had it was generous. The next day he returned again. I answered the doorbell. When I saw him I became annoyed and before he had time to speak I said: "Oh, you were here yesterday." His face was blank. I can still see it. He said nothing as I closed the door in his face. I came back into the kitchen and my sister, Maureen, said: "Sean, that was a terrible thing to do." It was only then I realized what I had done and I felt I had done it to the family of Joseph of Nazareth. What a fake I was in my clerical black.

And was not my earlier generosity shown up for what it really was—generosity to my own vanity? I promised God I would never again say "No" to a poor man who asked for help. I have not been faithful to the promise. On the other hand, trying to have a perfect record is something like trying to be God. If you refuse to make distinctions between the so-called "deserving" and the "undeserving" poor you will be found out very quickly by the con artists. It is difficult to continue giving to a con artist who returns again and again and does not even bother to hide the fact that he sees you as a very gullible person. But even a con artist has to live, and if he stoops so low to earn a living he is very poor indeed. It tries one's love precisely because there is nothing for one's vanity in helping him out. The blow to one's pride is much more painful than the drain on one's pocket. I told one such man he had overplayed his hand and he stopped coming back. I felt bad about it. If we love, money does not matter. It has value only in the moment it is given away. It is not what most people want. When God gives, it is himself he gives, not handouts. The point I am making is that there is a point, a line drawn, beyond which we are not generous with the gift of ourselves. Our love is limited and some of it is self-serving.

God alone is love. It is the inner essence of his being to be given away totally and completely. He accomplishes this first of all within himself in his absolute fidelity to the truth about himself. There is God himself, the Unoriginate Father, and there is the Word of the same God which is the Truth about himself, and the Holy Spirit of love which is his absolute fidelity. Basic to our "image and likeness" to God is our own fidelity to the truth about ourselves. And that truth is discovered when we give ourselves away. Our contemplative praying will consist in discovering that he has made his home in us, living his life through the medium of our life, loving through the medium of our loving and caring through the medium of our caring and sharing. He is given-away in our given-awayness. We are in God to the extent that we are given-away people. When God has given himself away there is only poverty left, the total poverty at the heart of God. The no-thingness, the givenness, the poverty and the love are all one and the same in God and in us. The only reliable sign of God's presence in anybody is the poverty of spirit of a given-away person. Doing things for people has its limitations. There is only so much one can do. Being given to them in one's inmost person need have no limitations. There has to be pain getting there. It is the pain of loss, darkness, spiritual disembowelment that is inseparable from apophatic prayer.

God has no shady areas, no corners of his make-up he is unwilling to share, no part of himself (if we may speak that way) that he keeps for himself. He has given himself to us and belongs to us. The difficulty lies in the simplicity of it all. We can no more see him than we can see ourselves seeing. Or to put it in another way, when we love in our deepest spirit we are not watching ourselves loving. When we love spontaneously, without thought of return or reward, we are having an experience of God. We may know later by reflection that he was there, that he is here, but we are so one with him that he sees through our seeing and hears through our hearing. We know him as beautiful in all that is beautiful, crucified in every pain, resurrected in everything that is good. He is at the center of the heart's anguish wherever people are opened out and seeking mercy. There is no other way to discover that he alone is the Meaning.

I went to court some years ago with a man I deeply love. He was known in the court as "the accused." A strange thing happened in the court that day. The judge in his gown, the secretary, the clerk of the court, the prosecutor and myself were very neatly dressed and very complacent and secure in our awful self-righteousness. The accused looked pretty seedy in an old suit of clothes, shuffling a bit with his arthritis and blushing. God, how I groaned inside for his blushes! The prosecutor announced: "The people of the state of X against the accused"—mentioning his name. I thought, "The people of the World against Jesus Christ." The accused was totally honest without a trace of resentment or even defensiveness. "Ah well, you know your Honor, I was in the wrong." He went on at length telling the judge of his feelings and compulsions. The judge allowed him to speak. I began to sense a new atmosphere in the court. His honesty was disarming in a very real sense. He was actually taking away the judge's power. His honesty was making him the judge of all of us. We were no better than he. We were just the phonies who had not been found out. He, being honest and sincere, was the truly good man. Suddenly the judge began accusing himself to the accused. He told of indiscretions of his own at an earlier period of his life. The judge, in the light of luminous honesty, saw himself as judged and passed judgment on himself. I was amazed. He didn't even know he was doing it. Later the prosecutor told me a long story about the time he was in trouble in the university and was helped by a Sister I knew. He also was passing judgment upon himself. It was then that I understood about Christ as the luminous and sincere given-awayness of the Father. He was made sin, as St. Paul put it, for all of us. In his luminous honesty before Pilate and on the cross he became, and remains, judge of all of us who had condemned him. He is to this day given away in the poor who have nothing, and his givenness is luminous love.

What to do

The whole person, the spiritualized body, prays.

Sit straight so that the blood may flow freely to the brain, the weight be evenly distributed.

Let your hands rest in your lap.

Close your eyes but keep in touch with reality.

Take a deep breath, fill up your lungs. Exhale slowly. This gets oxygen into your bloodstream. Exhaling enables you to relax. Repeat the deep breathing several times allowing the feeling of relaxation to go down through your body to your toes.

Focus your mind deep within yourself as when you are deep in thought.

Enter without discussion into God's presence at the center of your being. Remain there in silence. Bear up under the strain of maintaining silence.

If the mind wanders, recall it. Or repeat a word slowly such as "Father" or whatever helps you to concentrate and stay alert.

Allow your relationship with God to develop freely, ending with surrender and a word of praise.

3. The Poor Christ

It is not easy to grasp the idea of no-thingness. Yet it is something very positive, the ground of all things, the ambience of being. It is like the silence that bears the sound. Sound is not heard in sound but in silence. "When all things were in solemn silence, your almighty word leaped down from heaven."

The Father, the mysterious Other, revealed himself by sending his Word made flesh who said: "He who sees me, sees the Father" (Jn 14:9). It is understandable, then, that we should expect to see in Jesus the no-thingness, the given-awayness and the total poverty of the Father. St. Paul expresses it in II Corinthians, 8:9: ". . . he was rich, but he became poor for your sake, to make you rich out of his poverty." He did not say "to make you rich out of his richness," although that is the way we think, for the most part. Jesus is the way to live human life divinely. He has come into a world enclosed upon itself, a world its own pseudosavior, clawing its way to survival. It is a world of limited objects and "out there" objectified persons. The Wholly Other can not but be paradoxical in such a world. The Given-Away can not but expect incomprehension and rejection in a world centered upon itself. How can an enclosed world accept the challenge to become unselfish in disinterested love?

The poor Christ reveals the Father given in gift. The whole thing, from the viewpoint of practical common sense, could be looked upon as absurd. He who "sustains the Universe by his powerful command" (Heb 1:3), the Almighty God, is born in a stable. His "life-style" is that of a baby, so let us be realistic about it: God bombs his diapers. And stables stink. I know, because for years I cleaned out the barns at the abbey. The smell gets into your clothes and into the skin of your hands. Here is the great God in this situation—seemingly, if we honestly think about it, absurd. But to the Father it is not absurd. It is the vulnerability of gift-love, the poverty of God. If we are to walk in the Way which is Christ the demand is total, but we cannot accept it. We cannot deny the poverty of Christ, but we cannot accept it either, so we wriggle out of it by romanticizing it—the blue-eyed boy on the golden straw, the warm breath of the oxen and the angels strumming their harps. Reality, however, reminds me of a time I was kicked in the chest by a cow whose udders I was washing prior to milking. It sent me sprawling on the flat of my back. Had any archangel come by strumming a harp he'd have found a poor reception. To accept Christ is to accept the inner poverty at the heart of unselfish love and the outer simplicity that reveals it. However, in Jesus' case "he came to his own domain and his own people did not accept him" (Jn 1:11). He tells us that he did not have a place whereon to lay his head. He becomes a mirror that reveals our selfishness to ourselves, and because we do not wish to be poor with the poor Christ we must rid ourselves of him. This we do by turning away and enclosing ourselves within ourselves.

At the passion of Christ the Roman soldiers were more straightforward than we are. Perhaps it was because they had none of the theological casuistery of believers. This founder of a kingdom who could not produce his credentials was absurd. Poverty is absurd and the poor Christ an absurdity. So they crowned him with an absurd crown, put a reed scepter in his hand and mocked him: "Hail, King of the Jews!" We will not mock him, but we also find it difficult to accept his vulnerability. He was never more vulnerable, more given away, more a no-thing, more a fidelity to the truth about himself. "I came into the world for this: to bear witness to the truth" (Jn 18:37). "Without beauty, without majesty [we saw him], no looks to attract our eyes; a thing despised and rejected by men, a man of sorrows and familiar with suffering, a man to make people screen their faces; he was despised and we took no account of him" (Is 53:2,3). I remember something that happened years ago in Ireland. A young man killed a boy to prevent him revealing that he had been molested. The father of the boy was distraught with grief but instead of being angry

14

he bought a bottle of whiskey, went to the father of the murderer and asked him to have a drink. "Yours," he said, "is the greater sorrow." It may have been whiskey but it was Eucharist, Christianity, death to self in thought for another, the painful and agonizing refusal of defensiveness and revenge. This is the way to live human life divinely. It seems unreasonable because it transcends reason. It also transcends all the pretensions of professional holy people.

I liked Brother Henry and Brother Ferdinand. They are both dead now. What I liked about them was that neither one of them was capable of bearing a grudge. They could take a lot of abuse. Abuse, in subtle or not so subtle ways, is something you get a great deal of where men live in close contact. Given the human condition, this is understandable and unavoidable. They would, after a moment's confusion or perplexity, immediately respond with smiles, friendliness and kindness as if nothing happened. One might say that for them No-Thing had really happened. When people are truly humble, not just working at it, it is virtually impossible to insult them. There is nothing there to insult.

Both were quite eccentric. Eccentricity is a way of coping. But in a world of practical-minded people—and most Trappists are very practical-minded—eccentrics are a refreshment. Life was a celebration for them. It could not be lived out with the self-conscious stuffiness of practical-minded people, especially if such people were touchy. Henry would go out to work like a man going into combat. He would wear a World War II helmet, with a hammer and sundry tools hanging like grenades from his leather belt. He was short in stature and his impish grin revealed his optimism. He had a thorough dislike for bulls and he was killed by one of them. The bull pushed his crushed body out under the lodge poles.

Brother Ferdinand was a master-tailor, trained in Germany. He sewed all our clothes, not only the habit but also the funny drawers with the drawstrings at the waist and knees, and the shirts made out of semi-bleached flour bags with Purina written across our backs. Dressed in overshoes to the knees, carrying a cane and wearing a cork helmet suitable to the tropics, he went for his weekly walk. He was a perfect gentleman. Ramrod straight he would click his heels and bow when he met you. He would then go to a distant part of the property and enjoy a smoke, something forbidden to all. He had a certain inner freedom. On his return he would wander round to the front of the abbey where he would astonish female visitors by bowing

15

and kissing their hands. Love and freedom will have their day, monastic silence or not. In earlier days, in the Abbey of Gethsemani in Kentucky, he had been the community's baker. Kentucky is hot and a bakery there is an inferno. Ferdinand had the presence of mind to do his baking in the nude. He died slowly and with great gentleness, lingering on for months and cared for lovingly in the abbey infirmary. Henry and Ferdinand—they are the poor Christ, offered up, given away, with nothing to be proud of or possessive of except their God.

You will have noticed in the Gospel how those who were ready for the kingdom were just such people. They had arrived at an inner poverty of spirit that set them free. They were people who had nothing to be proud of. There was the sinful woman in the village who kissed Jesus' feet. There was freedom in doing that. Despised as a prostitute, she had found inner poverty of spirit. She had nothing to lose. Much was forgiven her because she loved much. The so-called Good Thief was a terrorist who acknowledged that he was receiving the just reward of his crimes. He also had nothing to be proud of. The tax-collectors, Levi and Zacchaeus, despised as extortionists and collaborators with the enemy, had also arrived at an inner simplicity, recognized Jesus and were received by him. The Good Samaritan of the parable, chosen as the model of Christian love, was despised as a heretic of mixed pagan and Jewish ancestry. He was so unclean already that, unlike those who passed by, he could afford to express his love for the wounded man left for dead. We are also called to arrive at this inner poverty of spirit, this inner nothingness and openness to Christ. Whether we arrive there as a result of our sins or as a result of our virtues matters not at all, provided we become poor with the poor Christ. Struggling through this becoming process with our eyes fixed on the poor Christ is a large part of our contemplative prayer.

What to do

Be seated, relaxed, recollected.
Bring before your mind all created things.
Discover some of your prejudices:

You like warm weather —— dislike the cold
You like butterflies —— dislike mosquitoes

You like rabbits	—— dislike rats
You like tropical fish	—— dislike snakes
You like some people	—— dislike others

But the things you dislike are all God's creatures doing what they are supposed to do. Some day you must make peace with them.

Project mentally toward them:
        sympathy
        understanding
        impartiality
        friendship

Remove the word "hate" from your vocabulary.
Become one with God's universe.
Surround it with your spirit.
Be poor toward all so that you may enjoy the luxury of
    loving all and being loved by all—All.

4. "The Bowels of His Compassion"

Awareness and alertness are characteristic of contemplative praying. Self-awareness is also necessary, although the gift of ourselves to others is what gives us personality. Self-awareness has a way of humbling us and teaching us our need for understanding and compassion. It is not the knowledge in itself that is important but its acceptance. To be able to accept the truth about ourselves is the work of love. Anxious frustration with our sins and limitations is the work of self-rejection and pride. Acceptance destroys pettiness and all attempts to be our own saviors. It sets us free and allows us to accept others. It leads us into an understanding of the humanity of Christ. There we see God and also see our own humanity.

The inner life of God, who God is, is translated into human flesh and blood, human experience, in the person of Jesus. Seeing him we see the Father. And what we see is a choked up compassionate love. In Luke 1:78 we read that through "the tender mercy of our God" Jesus, the rising sun, has come from the inmost depths to save us. "Tender mercy" is a possible translation of *diasplagkhna eleous.* I had always felt that the old translation—"Through the bowels of his compassion"—was a little crude. Now I feel that it is more to the point. *Splagkhna* are intestines and the compassion is intestinal, it is felt. When Jesus revealed the inmost depths of the Father, his inner mystery translated into human experience, it became an intestinal love, a love felt in the pit of the stomach, a lump in the throat, tears

18

in his eyes, and not simply a cool Platonic benevolence. It is a feeling-love, a groan of anguish that overflows in tears. This is God, the God who is discovered in our own prayer-life and in our history.

In Chapter 1 of St. Mark a leper comes and pleads on his knees: "If you want to, you can cure me." Jesus *splagkhnisteis,* choked up with compassion, touched him and said: "Of course I want to, be healed."

In Chapter 7 of Luke we read of Jesus entering the village of Nain. He meets a funeral procession, that of the only son of a widowed mother. Jesus identifies very much with the situation, being himself the only son of a widowed mother and headed toward death. *Esplagkhnisthae ep auto*—he choked up with compassion for her and gave her back her son.

He shed tears over Jerusalem (Lk 19:41). In Chapter 8, verse 2 of St. Mark, seeing the crowd, he said: "I am moved with compassion for all these people," the word is *splagkhnizomai.*

The same feeling-love is displayed at the death of Lazarus. He did not hide or suppress his feelings. He felt deeply for his friend Lazarus, but we find him with the practical-minded Martha carrying on a theological discussion about death—much as any one of us might do. Then Mary comes on the scene and she is crying. "At the sight of her tears" we are told, Jesus broke down and wept. How often have we not had the same experience. We can hold up until somebody else begins to cry and then our tears also flow. The fullness of life, if Martha knew it, was more than a theological discussion. John continues: "With a groan that came straight from his heart" he asked where they had buried him. The groan of compassion for others is part of the price that is paid for contemplative awareness. One could hardly accuse Jesus of being a sentimentalist, but sentiment is part of our compassion. Without it we become unfeeling people dispensing cold charity. "During his life on earth, he offered up prayer and entreaty, aloud and in silent tears . . ." (Heb 5:7). Those who saw the tears saw the inner mystery of God's love revealed in human form. We are never more divine than when we choke up with compassion for others. It may happen anywhere and should be recognized as a call to a prayer of love and oneness that "out of our poverty others might become rich."

When we are lonely we can learn much about compassion. Those are the times when we most need it. It would be a mistake to isolate ourselves from our loneliness by noise and idle activity. The presence of God may be the denial of loneliness, but then he is present more by his silence and absence than by any way he could be felt or experienced. Loneliness can of course be a trap for self-pity unless we reflect upon it.

I was a celibate for years before the thought even occurred to me that I might need others to complete my life. Celibate men can lead very isolated lives—functional, indeed, but with feelings submerged. There is the added drawback that, as our priesthood has been understood until now, we have "power" from the day of our ordination. It is power over people's conscience and it corrupts our hearts. Only a servant-ministry can free us. We have odd ways of coping with celibacy. I know a celibate who has a cabinet full of guns and shoots squirrels. Cardinal Spellman collected stamps. Others golf, build churches or harass the Sisters. I like to collect second-rate ideas and use my memory as a sort of scrapbook.

Loneliness is to some degree necessary. It has the capacity to put us in touch with the radical solitude which is at the center of our being where we are unique, alone, one of a kind. I came to experience the need for others through loneliness. I was chairing a discussion— we call them dialogues—on the possibility of our abbey and the region of abbeys opening a house in the Philippines. Monastic dialogues generate a lot of heat and some magnificent oratory. As I saw it, it was crystal clear that the Holy Spirit wanted a foundation in the Philippines. After all, the bishops there had been asking for one for a long time. Then there were vocations to our way of life but they had to leave the islands for places like Hong Kong, Indonesia, and America. On the whole, they had been unable to make the cultural change and were abandoning the life. It was obvious that they needed their own monastery, and I felt some sort of power of the Spirit to push it. I was magnificently fanatical about the whole thing. In my maverick fashion I was telling them that if they did not watch out they would find themselves in opposition to the Holy Spirit. This drove all the bats squeaking out of their belfries. The oratory shifted from their preoccupation with worries about financing the project and providing personnel to speculation on my stability, on my childhood relationship to my father and my need to see a psychiatrist. If you are not a little mad, of course, you will never get anything really creative done; so I was willing to concede the point about possible derangement, but it was missing the point. The work of the Spirit had to be done. I lay on my straw mattress those nights listening to them snore in the dormitory round about me. I had a funny feeling about how they could do it with such good consciences. One night in particular I had a mental image of myself as an insect somebody had stepped on and squashed. I thought that if there were only one person somewhere who accepted me even if not accepting a word I said, I would be happy. It was then it struck me for the first time that what I was asking for was a wife, somebody to be with me who would support me even if I were a failure. The insight was amazing. Until then I thought that marriage was for the most part concerned with as much sex as possible. With this new insight my depression left me because I knew now in some way what compassion was all about. I had no desire at all to run out and get married. My loneliness taught me that I needed others, that we could not just live or grow as spiritual, prayerful, ascetic robots with feelings suppressed or our abbey would be, as Sebastian Moore put it, a "collection of private wildernesses."

Incidentally, the foundation was eventually made and is flourishing. It was made as I had been suggesting on a volunteer basis; there were volunteers enough and money to spare. As it turned out, I happened to be the only volunteer turned down. Another thing I found out was that if you ever want to get a group of celibates to do anything, you must present it in a way that appeals to their starved vanity. Then they will sing like nightingales.

Compassion. I once saw an old priest with a lined face and snow-white hair weep at the funeral of another old priest, a friend of his. I knew that it was not self-pity. I was young then but knew enough to know that there was something God-like in it. I remember once seeing a young Sister who had nothing, borrowing a dollar from another Sister to buy a birthday gift for a third. They are the people who will be first in the kingdom, the people who have an ache for an incomplete world.

What to do

Become quiet.

For a moment accept yourself gently as a loving as well as a sinning person.

Allow yourself to be loved by God whose love is freely given, always available, ever faithful.

Hollow out a space within yourself and take into it all the suffering people of the world.

Recall them to mind: the sick, the blind, the deaf, the victims of violence, prisoners, people in mental homes, the lonely, the aged, those suffering from discrimination, the hungry, those with marriage problems.

Open your heart to them. Let them rush in on you and smother you. Let the compassion of Jesus be within you to welcome them. Pray to the Father out of their midst. Let the Spirit express your groan of compassion.

Be silent.

Afterward, go out and be gentle to people.

5. The Stranger

When we welcome a stranger, extending genuine hospitality and not merely a handout to an unknown and unexpected guest, what began with a simple act of courtesy becomes a faith-experience and an encounter with God. God is a stranger. Not being part of his own creation he cannot but be a stranger. For that reason any stranger is an apt symbol of God's presence, and provides us with the opportunity to welcome God in his person.

The day I left Ireland I said good-bye to my family at home. I did not want them coming with me to Shannon. That may have been unkind. It was not that I feared a scene of tears at the airport. It was that leaving Ireland was such a personal thing, like death, something I had to do alone. I had to be all together with myself to do it. In fact it felt worse than death. I would go on living without Ireland, without my family and friends and all the familiar things. That I might be coming to new friends and new experiences was of no help at all. I knew nothing of them. They did not mean any more to me than color does to a blind man. The plane, a four-engine Constellation, left late at night. All I remember of Shannon is the reflection of the lights glistening on the wet concrete. The flight to New York, with a stop at Gander for refueling, took twelve hours. I did not sleep. I was very cold in spite of two blankets, my own and that of my traveling companion who did not need his. We had both been ordained together and were going out to Fresno, California. I would have been glad if the plane had gone down in the Atlantic. But I knew it would not and it didn't.

We were strangers to America but we had relatives there. We had asked permission to spend a week in New York with them. Permission had not been granted by our diocese. So we spent twelve hours with our cousins and took another night flight to San Francisco with a connection to Fresno. Having survived my first cultural shock of being offered lemon instead of cream for my tea, I settled into another sleepless flight. It was humid and hot when we got to Fresno. It had been damp and cold in Ireland. I was limp like a wet rag from heat, jet lag and loss of sleep. The young priest who picked us up at the airport did not speak the whole way into the city. I tried to make conversation but it did not work. The grass, what little there was of it, was brown. The trees were a faded green. We were taken to the chancery office and asked not to remove our black suits and Roman collars because we were to meet the bishop. After a few hours of waiting we were shown into the bishop's office and our names were mentioned. The bishop continued writing at his desk without looking up. I wondered if this was a way of creating an impression or just that he didn't care a damn. With my loneliness and exhaustion I was in a very foul mood at this reception. In fact I was boiling. When he finally looked up he must have misread my appearance since he said, in an accent I was later to discover was Pennsylvanian, "Wha' ja scared of?" Glowering at him I replied, every word taut and clipped, "Bishop, I'm scared of nuthin.'" We knelt and kissed his ring. It was the thing to do in those days. He asked where I would like to work, in the city or in the country. I think he was trying to be conciliatory. But I was angry that he had not also offered the same option to my companion and I was in no mood anyway to be placated. "Bishop," I replied, "since I've never worked in either a city or a country parish, it's all the same to me where I go." He asked me to repeat it, which I did. He smiled. I was sent to the old Spanish Mission at Carmel where I was warmly welcomed by the people. I spent four very happy years there before an idealistic passion for an absolute made me join the Trappists.

When God is first encountered he is welcomed as a stranger. He "stands at the door and knocks." If anyone opens to him he will come in and sup with him. This is the contemplative experience. At unexpected times, in familiar or strange surroundings or events we hear the knock, open to the strange person, place or event. We share a feast of intercommunication and celebrate life with God.

All of this is worked out in very unstructured circumstances. What begins with respect for another ends by being a faith and salvation event. Had the door not been opened, the stranger not been welcomed, we would have missed God and never have known it. To the extent we welcome the other we welcome the Wholly Other. St. John writes: "No one has ever seen God; but as long as we love one another God will live in us and his love will be complete in us" (I Jn 4:12).

Abraham was a man of prayer. He listened to God who called him out of Ur of the Chaldees. He set out not knowing where he was going. He came through Haran to the Oak of Mamre where he settled. Sitting at the flap of his tent one day, he glanced up and saw three strangers. He welcomed them and modestly asked them to eat "a morsel." He then prepared a lavish banquet that revealed the depth of his hospitality. Suddenly, what had been a simple act of courtesy became an encounter with God and a salvation event. He was promised an heir, his descendants would be like the sands of the seashore. Lot welcomed the same strangers into Sodom. Again, what began as simple courtesy and hospitality to strangers ended by being a salvation event. Lot and his family were saved from the destruction of the city. Jacob, crossing the ford of Jabbock, wrestled all night with a stranger, asking that the unknown person reveal his name—in biblical language the inner essence of who he was. Wrestling with God in inner darkness, seeking his name, is much of what contemplative prayer is all about. That this is what Jacob was doing is clear from his later boast: "I have seen God face to face and have survived" (Gen 32:31). Contemplative praying can never be separated from one's experience of living life. It is not possible to get up and walk away from it.

The Israelites, conscious of having been strangers in the land of Egypt, wrote hospitality into their Law: "It is Yahweh who loves the stranger and gives him food and clothing. Love the stranger, for you were strangers in the land of Egypt" (Ex 22:20; Deut 10:18, 19). The tradition is continued in the New Testament: "Continue to love each other as brothers, and remember always to welcome strangers, for by doing this some people have entertained angels without knowing it" (Heb 13:1, 2). A stranger who just happened along had been hired by

Tobiah Jr. to be his guide. The stranger turned out to be the angel Raphael who saved his life.

The great welcome-a-stranger story in the Gospel is that of the two disciples on the way to Emmaus. Though dispirited, the disciples welcomed the stranger, listened to his words, and "the day being far spent" invited him to supper. They recognized the living Lord in the breaking of the bread. Contemplative awareness reveals Jesus in the stranger: "For I was hungry and you gave me to eat, thirsty and you gave me to drink, a stranger and you welcomed me" (Mt 25:35–38). Salvation is the reward given to those who welcome strangers. Matthew continues, speaking of those who welcome others: "Come, you whom my Father has blessed, take for your heritage the kingdom prepared for you" (Mt 25:34).

With contemplative insight we see God in the poor, in the people of strange faces and accents, the people of strange ideas, even in the aggressive and sinners. Any opening of the mind or heart to another is an opening to God and a salvation event. The strangers are the bearers of the God who seeks us.

Presence to God can be discovered in presence to others. A casual "good morning" or a purely business relationship brings about very little presence. Presence must be personal and dynamic. Personal presence means that people are concerned, that they care, laugh and weep and love together. Dynamic presence changes and transforms people. Christ's presence is not static. It changes us, making us who we really are. In the past, stress was laid on prayer forms that recalled the historical life of Jesus. His life was expressed in symbols such as the stations of the cross, the crib, relics of the cross, even thorns from the crown. The weakness in this spirituality lay in the fact that it was possible to be deeply moved by these symbols and yet unmoved by the presence of the resurrected Christ in our midst. A shift of emphasis has taken place. Christ as alive and resurrected is more apt to be honored today in the stranger, the neighbor. There is a new mysticism that sees the fourteen stations in fourteen hospital beds, fourteen shut-ins or prisoners or migrant laborers. Devotion to the crib is fulfilled in efforts to preserve the right to life because Christ is there. Personal and dynamic presence to Christ, mystical awareness if you will, is inseparable from presence to others. Wherever there are peacemakers—people hungering and thirsting for justice—or people who are merciful, who share, love, forgive, support, there Christ is present and at work. The contemplative with his or her intuitive approach not only sees Christ there but is caught up into a state of like-mindedness with Christ in his saving mission. People who work for the welfare of others need this insight.

What to do

Sit and be still.

Be present to the stranger within yourself.

Discover your uniqueness. You shall not be again.

Discard for now what you share with others—age, sex, weight, profession, race, religion. Say: "Not that, not that . . ."

Try to transcend within yourself all individual things.

You are an opening on the Infinite, a unique word God has spoken to this world.

You are a gift to the world which bears a message and love.

Surrender to that love and that destiny.

Silence.

Go forth and discover the uniqueness of others.

Uncover their uniqueness to themselves.

See the stranger as Word of God coming toward you.

6. Awareness

Out of presence comes awareness. Out of awareness comes vulnerability and availability to others. Presence activates the spirit making the moment spiritual. We act out of several layers of our being. At one time we act out of feelings—reason seems abandoned. At another time we act out of cold logic and feelings seem abandoned. At another time we act out of faith, which transcends reason and feelings though it may not abandon them. It is rare to find a perfectly balanced person who has integrated all levels, who acts as a whole person all the time. But when you do you are apt to have a problem—he may very well be a thorough and absolute bore. He can exude security like after-shave and is usually elected president of the board of directors. He is the obvious person to carry on business, civil or ecclesiastic, since he will never be tempted by wild mystical illogic, will never try to do the impossible or smash the unjust to smithereens. The world, somehow, seems to need dull people for the sake of neatness.

Awareness gives a compelling power, an edge of excitement to the simplest of activities. It brings the whole of one's inner life, deliberately and with precision, to bear on them. For example, it is one thing to shuffle into a room, another to walk in with a spring in one's step. Awareness of what we are doing makes walking become dancing, feelings become love, sounds become music, speaking become poetry and prayer, thinking become intuition, chores become sacred ritual and living become a celebration of God.

A contemplative approach to life demands that we be fully aware of what we are doing and of how we are doing it. For instance, if we even unconsciously consider ourselves superior to other people we shall be unable to be present to them. Asking personal questions as a means of showing how much we care is a patronizing attitude and is very insulting to poor people. It is a total want of presence. There can be no awareness and no presence to others where there is no active love. Love makes us the servants of others. So we must eliminate grasping in all its forms, no matter how subtle. We have to cease trying to capture God and others in our ego while we desire to stand at the center of the stage. We have to get rid of all self-importance and self-indulgence, all compulsive functioning of mind and body. Then we may find out that there are many ways in which we may be Christlike.

To be aware we must develop the power

to concentrate;
to be totally present;
to dwell on one thing, one word, one idea;
to have an accepting attitude to each awareness.

We have a habit of shutting out much, perhaps most, of the reality around us. We are highly selective people. We ignore what we consider irrelevant. But much of what we discard as irrelevant is very relevant did we but take time to be aware of it. Perhaps nothing is irrelevant to a person of prayer. Selection is a defense mechanism against the demands of reality. If we are so defensive in our relationships to things about us, how can we ever be aware of God or enter into his presence?

We have to expand both inner and outer awareness. Inner awareness is expanded by focusing the mind deep within, concentrating, while blocking out all individual things. This allows the mind to go down deep into the unconscious even to the ground of one's being where in fact there are no limitations or boundaries. One may have at first to face scattered impressions, disconnected images—we used to call them distractions—which are very much like dreaming. Facing them and letting them be without reasoning about them does in fact

29

fulfill the function of dreaming and settles or integrates our inner feelings. But if we persevere in our centered concentration we will go beyond those disconnected images and come to more lasting and archetypal images. They open us out beyond ourselves into the universal. They usher us into the presence of God, the ground of our being and of history.

The approach to the expansion of outer awareness is more direct. It is necessary since without it we shall be doomed to living very dull lives. We shall not hear because we do not listen. We stumble over things because we are not aware. To expand outer awareness we must look for the colors in unexpected places, listen to faint sounds, touch things, sniff the air, search for the dimensions of things and how they stand in relationship to one another. We have to be aware of people's body-language. We have to open our eyes and take a fresh look, constantly asking: "Why?" And especially we must ask the question, "What is the meaning of this in the context of God?" If nothing is pure chance, that is happening in some realm outside his providence, then it devolves on us to discover that providence. It will be God's ongoing private revelation of himself to us, his dialogue of love with us. In fact, there is no such thing as blind fate. The deeper understanding is available if we seek it, and the new insight will be enriching. This may seem to be a dangerous business, but most of the matters of our daily living are not that major, and in major matters you may find a director with whom you may sit down and discern the spirit.

I spent two years in a hermitage. From an unsympathetic point of view it may have appeared that I was playing god in my isolation. But at the time it was the thing I felt I had to do if I were ever to learn anything about prayer. And when we are sincere God does not allow us play god for very long. For as long as it lasted—two full years—it was a fairly genuine hermitage. The solitude was not only physical but also psychological since most of the community members did not approve of the venture. The building was a broken-down trailer home, eight feet by twenty-six, which we got for eight hundred dollars. It leaked badly. We hauled it up into the hills out of sight of the abbey to a place where I could hook up with the waterline and where I had a good view of the valley.

One of the first discoveries in the hermitage, perhaps known to all who live alone, is that while living with people one allowed them to occupy almost all of one's symbol-life. We are preoccupied with the interaction, with our thoughts of them and their thoughts of us. We project our personal feelings altogether too much upon them. They give us the feedback out of which we assess our lives. That disappears in the hermitage. The hermitage gave me a new awareness of nature and a new presence to it. Nature became my symbol-life and gave me the feedback I needed as well as special challenges not otherwise available.

The first awareness was that of being a creature amongst creatures. I realized that until I had begun to live in the hermitage I had been a little god in my own right with ideas I could push, projects to accomplish, a little kingdom of my own to dominate, a certain space nobody was allowed to occupy except myself. Now in the hermitage there were no people, no ideas to communicate, no projects. There were little things at first—a fence to build to keep the cattle at arms length, a rockery and an improvised splashing fountain; but then fall arrived and winter quickly behind it. I remember the honking of the wild geese as they flew south in the fall. They were a faint arrowhead so far up in the sky I could hardly see them. They spoke of freedom. Here I was, a thinking human person, a believing Christian supposedly free, yet confined of my own volition to a hermitage while they went south for the winter. I wondered what freedom was all about. It certainly was not license to do as I pleased. Nor did it mean that God would move in and overpower me. There had to be something of transcendence in it. That was where my eremitical experience was leading. An inner transcendence had to be found before an outer transcendence would be possible.

Winter was a succession of short days and long nights. I had a propane heater but no light. The snow was piled up all round and the silence was total. So were the loneliness and the meaninglessness. When March came the weather changed and a storm blew from the seventh to the seventeenth. The roof on the trailer house went "boom-boom, boom-boom" all day. I watched three containers as they collected the drips and I reflected on the Scripture passage that said, "A nagging wife is like a leaking roof." I was glad to settle for the roof. The booming of the roof prevented concentration and reading. For the most part I sat all tensed up at my desk. I would realize that I was tense and relax my muscles, but a short while later I would find myself all tensed up again. The solution was of course to get some rocks up on the roof, but it takes time to get round to such logical thinking. One day in the middle of all that I saw two wild ducks flying directly into the storm. The storm blew them up and backward but they fought it. They were heading for a little stream down in a valley to the left where they nested each year. They became a symbol of my necessity, my pigheaded perverseness in trying to do what to others was utter nonsense. The wild ducks flying into the storm could not have known, any more than I could have known, whether what they were doing would ever serve any useful purpose. That moment was its own purpose. Life is now. In the midst of the storm they opened me up to myself and enabled me to find peace.

I watched the squirrels and chipmunks freeze when the hawks screamed overhead. I saw the blood on the snow where the weasels killed the cottontails. I saw a snake holding on to a tuft of grass with his tail as he was being swallowed by another snake. Was nature cruel? Perhaps it was merely indifferent. I also was a creature. I knew nature could kill me. The aloneness opened up areas of fear deep within me. It was not just the fear of some physical thing happening, like my propane giving out on a sub-zero winter's night. That happened and it was ten below when I woke up at midnight. I had to get out of my sleeping bag and find my way down to the abbey. It was fortunate I woke up. But there was a deeper fear emerging from the depths of my spirit. It had something to do with the confrontation of survival with extinction, now that all the accustomed securities had been removed. Solitude is a fearsome thing. In the desert we meet our demons.

Nature would survive, of course. It would kill judiciously to do so. That also was its law. It had not arrived at love where one element of it could be aware of another's right to exist, and choose to lay down its life for the other. There were no rights. It would kill dispassionately but it would never be cruel. Only men mock before they kill and only men kill for pleasure. I wondered about survival. Is it such an absolute that it justifies war? Are there not greater values than the prolongation of life—one of them being love? On the other hand evil must be contained and love demands the protection of others. I was beginning to realize that the broken reed and the smoking flax had also their right to exist in the world. So when Tuck, my friendly squirrel, climbed up on my shoulder and sometimes sat on the top of my head I let him have his way. Together we would sit there motionless looking down the valley. Terribly unhygienic—perhaps he was the carrier of various diseases—and quite silly also. But I did not care much because my space was becoming his space also, and ultimately the space of other people who would enter my life. Harmony allows others to be others. It even allows God to be God without his having to spell it all out for us. Being aware of what is other, being present with one's spirit to it without wanting to possess it reveals our spirit to ourselves and God to ourselves.

What to do

There are two approaches, one direct, the other indirect.

1. Expand your awareness directly. Look about you. See the colors of things. Make a point of looking carefully at the areas you might be inclined to overlook. Everything has color. Be present with the whole of your being to the color of things and their various shades.

Now observe the shape of things. Look for lines and perspective and the harmony of their togetherness. If you had to draw the room in which you sit, how would you go about it?

Listen to the sounds. Identify all the various sounds you hear. Observe how they intermingle. Can you put them together into harmony, counterpoint, music?

Be aware of the texture of things. Touch them.

Now put all together, color, shape, dimensions, texture, sounds and feel present to the whole, feel what it means to be fully alive.

Move on. Be present to a person. Be aware of that person's history, struggles, successes. Be present to the uniqueness. Be conscious of the struggle of the whole human family, the struggle to be free, the upward movement of the spirit that resulted in art, literature, music, architecture, philosophy, law and love. Be present to God calling forth that spirit, originating love.

2. By departing and returning we arrive at a new awareness, a fresh look at a thing or a person.

Sit still, eyes closed.

Relax all your muscles, not directly, but by imagining what it feels like when they are relaxed. If this fails, tighten up your muscles one by one and then relax them.

Be quiet. Focus deep within yourself as when you are deep in thought. Go down into an inner room.

Drop all ideas, fantasies and symbols.

Come into God's presence without trying to objectify it.

Uncover an inner harmony, a sense of transcendence, a calm, a waiting in silence for nothing to happen. Hold yourself available.

Return refreshed after twenty minutes or so, more at peace with yourself and the world, more unified, more in harmony with God.

Do not pray with a mercenary mind, always expecting a reward.

7. Alone and All-one

Today's hermits and anchoresses for the most part live alone in apartments. Apart-ment is a very apt word for the experience. The question is: how can people live alone and not suffer the destruction of their spirit? It is estimated that there are 20 million shut-ins in America. Many live in retirement homes, virtually ignored by their families. Two or three million live entirely alone in apartments. Many celibates whose lives are dedicated to others live on the margins of society in apartments or rectories. The marginal aspect of their lives is more than physical. They are unable to buy into many of society's values. Their loneliness can be very real even though there are those who say that God is the denial of loneliness. We have to discover a spirituality and a prayer form to cope with loneliness and apartment living.

My eremitical experience was 90 percent loneliness and 10 percent a wild mystical joy in the goodness of things. As a relief from being alone I would have welcomed a visit from my bitterest enemy, had I an enemy. The second St. Patrick's Day was one of those lonely days. I sat inside the window looking down the valley. The snow was deep on the ground. I had been in the hermitage a year and seven months now. It was not easy to get down to reading or prayer. St. Patrick's Day in the abbey had always been just another Lenten day. There was no celebration. But at least in the abbey there were people and distractions. I sat there thinking of Ireland, its music and literature, its green hills and old castles and ruined abbeys. I thought of my parents and family and what they would be doing. The loneliness felt like a vacuum in my chest, sucking the life out of me. I fought self-pity. Later in the day I had to go down to the farm and one of my colleagues gave me a package wishing me a happy feast day and asking me not to open it until I arrived back at the hermitage. I struggled up through the snow, slipping and sliding but happy that somebody had thought of the day. I was of the impression that the package was a typewriter. It turned out to be a practical joke, a ten-pound lump of concrete. I did not cope with it very well. Being alone can kill the spirit. We joked about it the next time I met him. I felt that it was one of those things one has to undergo quietly as a growing experience, a moment not to be wasted.

Winter was long. I would rise at about 4 A.M. and spend three hours in prayer waiting for the sun to rise. I would watch where it rose and set each day, wishing for the days to get longer. There was such complete silence I could hear my heart beating. Then spring finally came. The days were warmer and there was more sunshine. I was outside one day and saw a trickle of water in the little creek that ran through the scrub maple trees. It was a sign that spring had arrived. I was so relieved that my eyes overflowed.

It may not be possible to avoid loneliness in solitude. We are social people. Nobody is ever entirely comfortable with being alone. But aloneness must become what the word really means—all-oneness with the world, with people and with God. Sensitive people can experience solitude and loneliness even in the midst of a crowd. Much of it arises from coming in touch with one's inner uniqueness, the mystery at the center of the individual that cannot be shared with anybody. It can only be submerged by noise and excitement. Solitude is a time of testing, not a call to isolation but an invitation to break down the walls of separation. It is not a time to sit staring at the four walls, to give way to an early senility or boredom. It is a call to contemplative prayer, if for no other reason than to discover that being alone is not the whole of one's reality.

There is an invitation in Scripture to go into one's inner room, shut the door and pray to God in that secret place. We are told that God who sees us in that place will reward us. Prayer heals the destructive element in solitude. It keeps communication and concern alive, preventing the solitary from lapsing into illusions or becoming a harmless eccentric. We are real to the extent we communicate. No one is more real than the person at prayer. When we pray—I am not thinking of saying prayer formulas—we are involved in a search for meaning, in the search for God who is Meaning; we are taken out of isolation in a movement toward God and others. We grow in love, and in that love for others our private illusory world collapses. People who love welcome other people into themselves. God and God's people are no longer distant from them. The ancient solitaries understood this and had a saying about being "never less alone than when alone."

There can be a deep sense of oneness with all people when alone and a deep sense of caring for them. This is not irresponsible neglect for their pressing needs. If we are convinced that prayer has a value, that it is a powerful energy for good in the world, then it is an apostolate, a form of ministry to others to which our whole strength may be dedicated. But solitude, if possible, should be temporary. The great masters of the contemplative life were distrustful of eremitism. Basil of Caesarea would allow a monk some time in solitude for one reason only—that he should learn to overcome human respect, take responsibility for his life and gain strength enough to make decisions. Having looked loneliness, which is a form of death, in the face the solitary will no longer fear God, man or the devil. Jerome, Augustine, Benedict and Bernard all had reservations. We need social contact as a corrective and as a stimulus in our lives to enable us to transcend our selfishness.

The element of all-oneness can also be found in liturgical worship in the hermitage. A daily eucharistic liturgy in a hermitage presents serious problems to a liturgist. The liturgy is a community celebration, the breaking of bread with others, the sharing of Christ's peace, the growth into the one Body of Christ. The liturgist would hardly be satisfied with my saying that during my liturgies I did not ever feel alone. Yet I was indeed in the presence of the whole of the human family. I performed, may I claim celebrated, the liturgy very slowly, pausing time and again to experience a deep unity with all the peoples of the world, then moving on again. There is more to the celebrating world than the mere physical presence of people. We celebrate many things at a distance, the establishment of peace, the election of a pope, and we experience the event deeply. The liturgy was not my own, not a pious and private devotion. For one thing I was surrounded by nature which is part of our life history, an extension of ourselves. The mountains, the sage, the elk, the chickadees were all a living chorus of praise to God. I was not more nor less than any one of them. I too was only one of God's creatures but the one with intelligence who could voice their praise to God. It was a very humble service I performed on their behalf. On Easter Sunday morning, when the Resurrection was exploding inside me, I came to know what Isaiah experienced. I felt compelled to look up at the Wasatch Mountains to see them skipping like lambs, and listen to the water in the creek clapping its hands. In a manner of speaking they really were doing just that. There is a kinship with nature when the barriers are broken down. Having nothing we come to possess all things and loneliness is turned into a wild joy. In solitude we fluctuate from aloneness to all-oneness, from loneliness to joy and back again.

There is a shock element in solitude. Familiar relationships end. Our day is spent with things rather than with people. We have no influence, nothing so pressing we must get it done. Can we "be" and be happy? Is it sufficient to be who we are without the necessity of being busy? The whole negative side of things looms large in solitude, no word of praise or encouragement, no help, not even the corrective protest of people's silence to enable us stay alive. Then there is a trial of faith that asks if anything is real except what can be seen or touched. It is a painful loss of godliness.

But there is a positive side to solitude. It is a contemplative experience. In apart-ment we do not go to God through pious practices and exercises, though some of them need not be ruled out. Prayer in solitude is positive but with a passive aspect. It consists in holding one's emptiness and nothingness open to as direct as possible encounter with God. One's time in solitude is experienced as holy time, sacred to God and not to be idled away, *chronos* transformed into *kairos*. Each moment is filled, not with things to be done, but with the positive holding of one's whole person open to welcome God. One has to "be" someone rather than do something, be a child of the Father in the Father's Son. Nothing happens usually, and yet something happens—we change. We are no longer set over against the Father to whom we might pray, as it were, over an impassible chasm. We rest in God, not called upon to do anything in order to communicate with him. He does his being in our being, thinks himself through to us through the medium of our loving thought, compassionates all people through the medium of our compassion and our loneliness. In our solitude we would be nobodies were God not with us. It is in this very emptiness itself of apart-ment living, emptiness of goods, projects, people and meaning, emptiness that has no meaning for practical, pragmatic people, that God is found. We have empty hands. More difficult still, we have empty souls. We see ourselves as creatures and sinners, empty of any strength or virtue, and we wait day following day for God to fill the emptiness. But we are glad now that we are empty and have nothing in which we might take pride. Our hands are winter branches lifted to a night sky. Everything is dark. But he is not "out there." To look out there is to separate ourselves from him. He is at the deep center of our empty "where," gazing his full fill on all the extensions of our existence. Our faith is filled with the reality of his presence as we hold our empty hearts open to him. In our sense of loss it does not matter now. It is good that we are empty, and we shall continue empty even after we have found everybody. His absent presence is fullness, absolute love, absolutely loveable, utterly transcendent yet immanent. He himself is the emptiness; the loneliness is his transcendence. He is the healing, the nothingness and the All. He shares his concern for people with us as a friend would with a friend. We remain who we are and what we are, alone yet present to everybody, empty but without any need to approve of ourselves. We are terribly lost yet found, confined but inwardly set free. And this freedom is our joy.

What to do

Be seated, relaxed, very silent inside, alert.

Enter into your solitude.

Turn away from all peevishness and fretting. Let this moment take care of itself and be its own purpose.

Deepen your awareness of how you have already been graced. You are a child of the Father in Christ. Your body is a temple of the Holy Spirit. The Trinity has made its home in you. The kingdom of God is within you. Your center is an altar on which pure prayer is offered to God. Your life is liturgy.

Have a sense of awesome respect for the God who favors you with his love. Do not take it for granted.

It ennobles you. Have a sense of your nobility, of your intrinsic worth, a sense of quiet self-assurance.

Let your need to be loved draw God into you.

Enter the silence and wait without discussion.

Surrender to the unseen presence . . . "into your hands . . ."

End with a word of praise.

8. Watching and Listening

I developed some basic animal skills in the hermitage. Watching and listening were two of them. Even when I gazed, unfocused, down the valley I found myself taking in the whole scene. If a twig moved off to the left or to the right I would immediately notice it and, without movement on my part, want to know what it meant. I would listen constantly. Even when deep into reading I would never stop listening, identifying each sound—the wind, the song of the red-wing blackbird or kill-deer or chickadees, the cry of a hawk, the snuffling of the cattle as they searched for grass amongst the sage, the splashing of the fountain. After some months a new sound would jar the whole harmony of the place, leaving me with a sense of unrest or fear until I could place it. The concentration involved in motionless watching and listening is intense, but the curious thing about it is that it is not a distraction. It does not take one away from what one is doing. Actually, it sets the mind free for prayer. Distraction arises when we reason. Like the animals who are not involved in the reasoning process it is possible to be deeply concentrated in listening and watching, but unlike them with one's intuitive faculties wondering, open, receptive. Prayer is not a time for reasoning.

The wildlife began to accept me because I did not speak, nor did I make any sudden moves. In the early morning the sage hens would do a very extraordinary sort of square dance on the little lawn I had built in front. A circle of ten or so of them would flap their wings, spread their pointed tail feathers into fans and prance into the center and out again. Weasels, which are much given to curiosity, would sit up straight, with their pointed faces and beady eyes darting from left to right, taking in the whole scene. The fat squirrel I named Tuck was the first to come. Then came a chipmunk. It was a good day when I could finally stroke his striped back with a finger. Boris referred to them as the "vermin." Boris really wasn't his name, but he was affectionately called that after a famous movie star. On my Sunday morning visit to the abbey he would ask with concern: "Do you really mean you allow them into your house?" For some reason or other, perhaps hygiene, it bugged him that I cared for the wildlife. Bugging one another is a form of entertainment brought to a fine art by enclosed religious people. It is not taken seriously either by the bugger or the bugee, unless, of course, you consider its therapeutic value. It is a safety valve and it challenges people to stay honest. Enclosure builds tension and there are various ways of coping.

I fed walnuts to Tuck and his friends. Tuck would wait rather impatiently, chattering his teeth, until I gave him a sign. Then he would hop up on to my knee and eat from the palm of my hand. I could not feed him from my fingertips since, for some reason, he would bite them. It seemed that he could not distinguish between my fingertips and the walnuts. Had he been human he would have been a theologian. I stole the nuts from the honey department on my weekly visit to the abbey. Bart was in charge of the honey, sort of whipping it up into cream so that it could be spread on toast. Walnuts and artifical flavors were added to give it personality. Bart had a round cherubic face with a look of innocence. He was very devout but it would have been a serious error of judgment to have asked his permission to feed his walnuts to the beasties.

There was a very venerable white-haired old man who fed crumbs to the birds while he held a rosary in the other hand. That was considered edifying. But it did not last. He was in the infirmary and got into a scuffle with another old man who was in there with a heart condition. The other man had a "thing" about electric appliances—I would call it a kinship. It involved him in considerable hammering as he installed outlet after outlet to accept the plugs. The white-haired monk wrote him a note asking him to hold down the noise. The note was not well received. In fact it led to some pushing and shoving that did not go unnoticed. The next day the white-haired man was given an airline ticket and told go to another abbey.

He never returned. He was a man who was all soft inside. I missed him. I have heard that he still fed the birds for years afterward.

The point in all of that—the squirrels, the birds, the walnuts and the people and so much more, has to do with watching and listening. It is not simply a matter of externals but of spirit in the affairs of life. Once we grasp the poverty of God as the love and givenness and holiness of God, we can grasp the theology and spirituality in the poor and simple things of daily living. God is not a clean objective idol that abstract intellectualism can make of him. Mystics have known him as a person, awesome, sublime, thrice holy, and weeping, forgiving and gentle to his people. He is also the God of joy. Could you imagine God not having a sense of humor, a gentle sense of the incongruous in the world he loves? He is the source of all things, and he is their spirit and much more.

Contemplative prayer is a form of listening—the Latin word for listening being *audiens*. We act *ob audiens* (obedience), that is, because of listening. Obedience to God is listening to God. The only alternative is to act out of a refusal to listen, *ob surdus* (absurd), out of deafness. The one who fails to listen to God is absurd. We learn to listen to God by listening to others. My earliest recollection is of listening to my Father and then deciding for myself what to do. I decided not to do what my Father suggested and he was not offended. He was not the sort of man who imposed his will on others. I was three years of age at the time. We were in the process of building a new home and were up there one day while construction was going on. Dad had shot a rabbit and was holding it up by the hind legs. It seemed as large as myself. He asked me to take it down home. He said it was all right, that the rabbit was dead and would not harm me. I did not understand what "dead" meant. I thought within myself: "You know that it will not harm me but I do not know that, and so I cannot take it." I refused, although of course I never spoke a word. The incident left a deep impression. Even to this day I cannot be sure whether this first conscious and deliberate decision was a sin emerging from a failure to abandon my independence in trust to my Father, or a mature act of responsibility, having listened. At any rate, my favorite symbol of my Father in heaven is that of my Dad as my brother Michael and I walked with him to school. He was a teacher. On rainy days he would open his coat and take us inside it, one on either side of him, and we would walk along with our ears close to his trousers pockets. On fine days he would point out the skylarks to us as they hovered way up in the sky. Their song was a marvel.

To listen with trust is to accept the Father's word. His final word is the Word made flesh, Jesus of Nazareth. God speaks to us. His Scriptures are not so much a source of information as a word that demands a response. The Bible is not read to satisfy curiosity but to uncover a call and respond to a person, God. He sends out his word. It always accomplishes what it was sent out to do: ". . . The word that goes forth from my mouth does not return to me empty, without carrying out my will and succeeding in what it was sent out to do" (Is 55:10, 11). The word passes judgment. It forces a decision. If we accept it, it changes us. Outright rejection or indifference, which is a form of rejection, results in what St. Jerome said: "Ignorance of Scripture is ignorance of God."

A person's word is a projection of the person himself. It is a symbol expressing the inner being of the speaker. To accept the word is to accept the speaker and much more. The word releases some form of psychic energy in us. If it is a good word we begin to trust, love, wonder, rejoice. If it is a bad word it releases anger, sadness, disgust or distrust. God's word is a good word releasing all that is best and most creative in our spirit. It calls us. God knows better than we do that nobody can be commanded into holiness.

The prophets of the Old Testament were men whose personalities were invaded by the personality of the word of God. People of prayer today who listen to the word in Scripture are invaded with the spirit and personality of Christ. When Abraham, Noah and Moses listened to God he made covenants with them for the sake of his people. Isaiah, Jeremiah and Ezechiel were hearers of the word for others. The word spoken in the solitude of their hearts was spoken for all the people to hear. The energy released was released for others. This is true of Peter and Paul, Benedict, Bernard, Francis of Assisi, John XXIII, and Mother Teresa of Calcutta. No gift is ever given that is not intended for others, for a few or for many. The renewal of the life of faith flows from those "who hear the word of God and keep it" (Lk 11:28). Jesus is the foundation of all contemplative listening. It is he who listens to the Father. Fundamentally, then, it is his Body the Church which is contemplative. Within the Church, and always for the Church, contemplative listening erupts in the individual. For that reason we have to be objective in our listening, not picking and choosing but hearing the whole message, prepared to hear the unexpected. Picking passages out of context to prove our predetermined positions is very wrong. To listen is to be alert to what the Spirit is saying to the world today. Contemplative listening enables us to discover Christ working in all his people. Listening opens our minds, brings awareness and understanding. It allows something of the spirit of Christ to enter us. Our interests, love and concerns become more universal. Through watching and listening, the word of God gets through to us and that word accomplishes what it sets out to do.

What to do

Choose a passage of Scripture.

Read it in a wondering fashion, mulling over it rather than studying it. Each word is important. A word you might easily overlook may contain the whole message you need.

Keep your reasoning out of the way so that God's ongoing revelation, personal to you, may erupt within you.

Be present to the Speaker in the word without putting words into his mouth.

Put aside the book and enter the silence.

Trust the word the Father speaks in your inner heart.

Surrender.

9. Times

Prayer is not an other-worldly activity, nor is it a purely mental activity. The whole person prays, the person as set down in time and space who is part of the whole time/space situation. When we define time as "a non spatial continuum" it does not tell us very much. But when it is defined or described as "the mode of becoming of finite freedom, in bodily form, personally and selectively realizing the potentiality of one's own being, attaining the unique irrevocable completion of its institution" we are left breathless. Time is measured by change, becoming, movement. It has something to do with the presence of death within life. Death is not the end of time but movement into the fullness of time where nothing is lost and death exists no more. What happens in our dying daily within time will be the content of our fullness.

A few weeks ago I went down to the South Fork of the Clearwater River where the pines step down the slope to the water. The sound of the water rushing over the rocks quiets the mind and brings an inner openness and freedom. But that day I had a distraction. I had been of the opinion that I knew what a river was. It was water running down to the sea—something very simple. Now as I gazed on it I realized I did not know at all what a river was. If the river was running water then it had already gone on downstream. It was doing just that, and yet there it was still with me. And the river certainly was not the riverbed. I looked upstream and followed the water with my eye, but the river always escaped me and went on down to the sea. I stood up and began to walk with it. It became my companion as I got to know its ways and moods, its darting and swirling, its calm and reflections. There was more to it than could be discovered at the point where I had been sitting. But then it struck me that the river was still back there where I had been sitting. I returned and sat down. I decided to look at it obliquely, with the hope of discovering its secret. The power of oblique thinking, thinking round something or thinking the opposite of it, will sometimes reveal the meaning where direct thinking fails. Perhaps the method would work with looking. I fixed my eye on a rock in midstream and concentrated. Suddenly the river stood still and the rock and river banks began to move upstream. I was onto something now. If the water stopped it would cease to be a river. It would become a stagnant pool. The river had to cease being where it was in order to remain where it was. This was very exciting. The river had to change constantly to maintain its identity. It had to undergo an unceasing death to remain alive. It was the biblical thing of losing one's life so as to save its real meaning. We must keep moving.

I got into the car and drove home. The road and the broken yellow lines came rushing toward me. That at least was my visual experience. I recalled a day in my youth when the whole family drove to Lough Talt, a little lake in the Ox Mountains the other side of the Windy Gap. We would go there on picnics. My youngest brother, Brendan, began to cry and we were unable to quiet him. "The trees," he said, "are running away." Of course they were running away. Here were the telephone poles and fence posts rushing toward me and running away. Trees in the distance seemed small but as I came toward them they suddenly grew and shot upward into the sky and rushed past me. It was contemplative gazing before dull reason was brought in to destroy the mystery and narrow the possibility of insight. To know them I would have to stop them, but if everything stopped perhaps everything would reveal some other mystery.

I sat in my room in prayer. I thought things would be quiet there. When I take a special time for prayer indoors I like to sit on a cushion in a semilotus position with my back against a hot radiator. As I sat there I glanced around the room from the Rouault print of the Judgment of Christ on the wall opposite me to the cluttered desk at my left. I suddenly realized that as far as my mind was concerned it really did not matter whether my eye crossed the room or the room crossed my eye. In either case my mind would have had the same experience. For that reason it mattered not at all whether I stopped my eye or stopped the room in order to focus and know. When the action stops we "know." Freeze the movement in the ant hill and you can study the ant.

The mind is an ant hill. I realized that my mind was flitting about from object to object, or equally that objects were flitting across my mind. I could not know unless my mind stopped long enough to focus. That was it. If my mind stopped, time would stop and the world would stand still. I remember the moment, in deep recollection, when the room stopped. I was amazed. I had not known that it had been moving. In deep centering on God the mind stops and one knows something about God, or rather God is known without one's knowing what is known. One knows the person. Time, measured by movement, comes to a standstill and one knows the fullness. When the room stopped, God was present.

Although I have a distaste for all forms of physical exercise and consider walking a form of violence, I infrequently go for a stroll up the hill through the pine trees with the purpose of keeping in touch with the lighter side of God. It was on one of those occasions that I realized that I did not quite know what walking was. As a means of getting from here to there it was less than attractive. And then I was well aware that in the experience of contemplative prayer the "sublime" was the means of getting from here to there. A door is not a hole in the wall. Its threshold is the dividing line between here and there. The word *limina* in Latin being threshold we come *sub limina* when we come to the threshold. *Sub limina*—sublime—the dividing line that allows us to look out "there." The sublime opens us up to gaze on the transcendent. It opens us to gaze on the mystery of God. The Jewish mystics would say that "beyond the mystery is the mercy," which, in fact, for us is the incarnation which brings me back to my contemplative stroll. I was wondering about walking.

Was walking really a succession of steps or not? I was still intrigued at the time by the whole thing about movement and change as measures of time in which, as the theologian put it, I was "personally and selectively realizing the potentialities of my being." If step two really followed after step one then it would simply be another step one. I looked down at my feet and wondered what I was doing. I took one step and stopped. It was simple. That was one step. I took another step, but it also was one step, except in the mind of a mathematician who deals in figures. But walking is something else. Only another step can come after a step one, but step two comes out of the death of step one. This is movement, not mathematics. As I walked I was unable to say where step one ended and where step two began. Step one died into the presence of step two. Step two came out of the dying process of the first step, not after it. A plane flew over. Its journey across the sky was constantly dying. The destination would not be reached after the journey ended. The journey would die into destination. The very death of the journey would be the emergence of the destination. Resurrection is not something that happens after death. We are dying into Resurrection which is the destination that wraps up the whole journey.

I sat at the top of the meadow looking across at the Breaks. The whole movement of dying and rising, the measurement of time and life, came before my mind. Races migrating, civilizations rising and falling, exodus, pilgrimage, Mohammed and Mecca, Moses and the Promised Land, the Latter Day Saints and Salt Lake City, Mao swimming the Yangtze were all caught up into Jesus' return to the Father. All are urged on by the inner truth expressed by Augustine that our hearts are restless until they rest in God. Newman put it: "To live is to change, and to have lived fully is to have changed many times."

What to do

Experience the transrational mystery of death and resurrection in walking or driving.

Reflect on change and becoming in your life.

Draw a faith-line, graphing the ups and downs in your life—notable decisions and experiences forming an upward movement, bad times forming downward strokes thus:

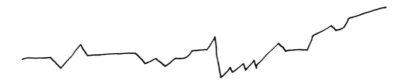

This is a symbol of your life. Accept it as graphed. Discover what it might tell you of your ability to bounce back.

Trust in further becoming.

Surrender the past, present and future to the Father.

Praise him for the support that enabled you to survive.

10. Spaces

Space is "the intuitive three-dimensional field of everyday experience." There is much more to space than can be measured mathematically. That much more is spirit. The spaces define the spirit or character of a thing or a place. In somewhat the same way, the spaces that lie between our experiences and our decisions define who we are and what character we have.

The spaces between the notes define the spirit of the music. Change the spaces and what was a waltz becomes a march. A long drawn-out note or sound, like a foghorn, has no personality. But lie in bed on a foggy night by a busy seaport and listen to the durations and levels of many foghorns and you will have atmosphere, spirit, character—the lonely sounds of ships lost in the fog. A symphony is created by spaces, the short notes and the long, the high and low notes, adagio and allegretto. But a symphony is much more than any random collection of notes. The composer puts his own spirit on the notes and they speak back to him. Rather than experience the music as such it is much better to experience what the composer experienced in his spirit when he wrote the music. Spaces and densities are basic to any work of art and are the bearers of its spirit.

I sit here looking at a pine tree outside my window. At first glance all pine trees, or at least all of the same species, look alike. We look at them but we do not see them. In fact, no two are alike. To see the tree we must look intently, concentrating on the spaces between the branches. It is not the branches but the spaces between the branches that define the personality of the tree. It takes a little time. We must focus and hold. The tree does not yield up its secret easily. The secret is really our secret. We put our spirit on the tree, much as the composer does on the sounds, and it comes back to us changed. We become what we contemplate. Eventually, and this is a consoling or a frightening thought, we become like the God we contemplate, the God of love or the punishing guardian of the moral law. We take the tree into our spirit and it quietly reveals its own spirit—"you alone are the one who cares to know. I was not and I am, and now that you know me I shall never cease to be. I am part of your fullness forever. To a logger I am only money, to an artist I have aesthetic value, to another I give shade or warmth in his furnace. But to you I am a word of God. This is the inner essence of my being. When he fashioned me out of nothingness I was modeled on himself. In some small way he had to be like a pine tree for a pine tree to exist. I am a word he speaks in trunk and branches and spaces. And he is like splashes of color and sunlight glittering on water. He is the sounds and the music and the laughter. He is storm and lightning, night and day, buttercup and tropical fish. They are his word as he unceasingly fantasizes them into existence from the depths of his being. They are because he is, and he holds all things in the hollow of his hand. All things mirror him." This is a little of what the tree says as it bends down and embraces me with its branches. To say that it actually does that, that it actually speaks would involve us in magic. But not to see or hear anything would leave us blind and deaf to the reality round about us, doomed to isolated and uninteresting lives. And once we grasp the personality of only one tree, then all trees get into the act and reveal their own uniqueness to us.

I went walking through the pine trees the other day. This time I was gazing on the spaces between the trees. I went past the cemetery and the rock quarry, up past the cabin and round the back way to come out at the top of the meadow. It was a quiet walk, watching the distant trees move past one another, constantly rearranging themselves as I went along. I passed what I call the Pietà—a large tree broken at the roots and lying over in the arms of two of its companions, then passed the Trinity tree, three trunks from one set of roots. A deer got up from the underbrush and went threshing up through the trees. He has been there all year. A coyote stood at a distance and watched me, but then left quietly with his head down. Coyotes have no reason to hold their heads high in our state. Yet it is pleasant to lie in bed at night and listen to their magnificent love songs, their mockery of rock-and-roll.

The spaces between the trees define the personality of the forest, ". . . and I have miles to go, and promises to keep." An orchard is functional. It is a product of mere reason. It has neither spirit nor personality. The spaces are equidistant, the trees trimmed to look alike. Were it large enough, we might get lost in an orchard—all points looking alike. We get lost in pure reason but we find ourselves in transcendence. The forest is not unreasonable. It transcends reason, which is why we find ourselves when we stroll there. Nobody in his or her right mind would go for a stroll in an orchard. The spirit of the forest is closer to our spirit than is that of the mutilated bodies and environment of the commercially cultivated fruit trees. But I was amongst pines and they stood on their roots. They have a tradition on this hill. Most stood tall, but a few, that could not bear the weight of winter's snow, were bent though still alive. Those that stood together trimmed each other clean. Those that stood alone had another beauty with branches reaching out in all directions. Others had fallen and lay surrounded by their companions as they slowly moulded back into the earth. The spirit of the forest is awesome and sublime. It mocks the pettiness of our lives. But even our lives have spaces, spaces in human affairs. They are the nontemporal moments when thoughts die into decision, decisions into act. They form our personality.

The finite is complex. It is easily fragmented. Contemplative awareness can hold it together. It draws together all the powers of our spirit and body to center on the deepest level of our being where God, the ground and the source of being, is present as gift and salvation. In quiet contemplative praying fragmented people are put back together again. Back at the time when I was pushing the idea of opening a monastery in the Philippines I was, myself, a very fragmented person. I was being told that I never ceased being a diocesan priest and that I should return. I was torn apart within, not knowing what to believe. There was nobody who could give me a sense of direction or say: "Look, this is all part of being a monk." I am not given to superstitious signs, but there is a certain harmony of things that to the intuitive mind indicates a way to go, a time to make a decision. I did not have that harmony, and there was no indication that any decision would be a step forward. I spent weeks in prayer, nights in nightmares. We have this conceit in the Trappists that our way of life is the ultimate in human endeavor, and that flunking out is a regrettable failure. We put a great deal into the life and leaving it is traumatic. Eventually, I wrote to my former diocese and was invited to return. I had been eighteen years in the Trappists.

I put the letter on the bulletin board, mentioning the day and time of my departure. A few said "good-bye." I was standing in the cloister as they passed by on their way in to Vespers. Most did not notice but it would not be true to say they did not care. Survival, much more than contemplative abstraction, has a way of leaving people preoccupied. I followed several down the cloister, tapping them on the shoulder and making my farewell. One replied: "Ah well, there were some good things about you." I was so low this condemnation by faint praise actually picked me up. We are funny people.

I spent four months in the diocese before I came crawling back again, but it was a learning experience—full of spaces, one might say. For one thing I was unable to drop my identity as a monk. I might be all screwed up, but I knew who I was and I was unwilling to be something else. I could not even dream of developing an identity as a diocesan priest. My former companions in the diocese were Monsignors which, for some reason, I felt was ghastly. The thought of a small country parish, counting the collection, paying the insurances and the whole bit was something I knew I could never do. With that frame of mind and fresh out of the enclosure, I was a sitting duck for an emotional involvement with the first woman who took any notice. That is putting the whole thing nicely. I began to drool over a statuesque blonde who had the proportions of a "wonder woman" and intelligence thrown in for good measure. Without going in to the bizarre details of my advances, it is sufficient to say that the bottom line was that she was gay, held all men in low esteem, including myself. The experience cured me once and for all of any thoughts that I might ever marry. Shortly after that, I was in a bookstore one day glancing over some things on witchcraft—it was a new subject on the shelves since I entered the abbey—and had reached up to take a book from an upper shelf when the words went through my mind: "You could go back to your abbey, you know." I pushed the book back on the shelf, returned to the rectory and called the bishop. He was annoyed and let me know it, but he gave me permission to return. He could not have done otherwise since he had not as yet officially incardinated me into the diocese. I departed the following Sunday and met my abbot at the San Francisco airport. He was flying out to the Philippines to accept a gift of property for the new foundation. I drove back to Utah in a new Nova I had bought. Flunking out was humbling but flunking back in was much worse. The prior panicked, called a meeting of the council and sought to have me confined to the guesthouse. It didn't work.

They did not have any particular job to give me. However, the procurator at the time told me that he did not have anybody to spray the alfalfa fields with weed killer, since it was blowing back in their faces and they feared contamination. I took the job, driving up and down the fields. It did blow back right into one's mouth and nostrils but there are worse things in life. The practical minded amongst the monks immediately traded the Nova in for a new pickup. A couple of weeks later I was driving this pickup down to get the mail. When I arrived at the crossroads a girl in white shorts cycled past, and while watching her I ran into another pickup coming from the right. It seemed to me that there was some sort of hidden message there—about the pickup, that is—not about the way the wicked world corrupts a monk who spends some time in it. For some strange reason I was glad to see the pickup get it. That was my corruption. As for the world, it is a beautiful and redeemed work of God, a new creation.

Fragmentation occurs when something finite occupies the space of another finite. Plant an acorn in a flower-pot and it will grow up to destroy the pot. If we impose our ideas, however good and true they may be, on others we shall destroy them. At best we may only serve one another's interests. God is utterly simple. When he enters our life he does not occupy our spaces, impose himself on us or dominate us. He is the real meaning of our life. He does not absorb us but brings to perfection who we really are. Through his presence, when we are most human and most loving, we come to know who we are. The human condition with all its complexity has gone in to God in Christ and is forever saved. The very human condition itself is sacramental of his presence. Accepting our humanness we accept Christ, and in accepting him we fragmented people are put back together again. The acceptance of the happenings and the outcome of our decisions—which are our spaces—is the restoration of harmony, the peace of Christ.

The spaces activate the spirit in our lives. To celebrate life we must put our spirit on it, have it enriched and returned to us. In the process it will save whatever receives and returns it. A thing, or for that matter a person, is only a thing until it is invested by spirit and discovers its transcendence. We are only intelligent organisms until we realize spirit in transcending ourselves. Spirit is intangible and invisible but very real. John F. Kennedy's rocking chair is kept in a museum—the heaven of rocking chairs. There it is dusted, protected and honored. It is saved. One could have gone downtown and found a better chair, a more expensive one with gadgets and more class. What J.F.K.'s rocking chair has is spirit. This is the chair on which the President sat while making decisions of state. He has given it something of his own spirit. It is not just any chair, and yet no scientist can demonstrate what it is that makes the difference. People come from afar and look at it. It has acquired a sort of salvation because it is more than it appears. Log cabins in which famous men were born are preserved by the State as monuments. They have a quality, that special spirit given to them by the person who was born there. It transcends the building itself and saves it while skyscrapers are torn down. There are times and places that are special to us. It was there or at that particular period in our history that we were challenged to grow and transcend ourselves, to make a special effort. We put our spirit there and there it was mirrored back to us.

When the old confessional was torn down to make way for one more suitable to the new rite, I had a very strange experience. I had never given any thought to the old one, but on this particular day at dinner I had an urge to go up and look at it. The front of it was all torn off. I had a feeling as if it were dying. Then for one intense moment of intuition I experienced the whole life or spirit of the confessional, all the sad stories told there, the tears and hopes, the struggle to rise and do better, the relief when people were reconciled and made whole again. It seemed as if I had to be there to receive its spirit and allow it die into me and be part of me forever. I now know that everything that exists is not only a word of God but is also seeking a savior into whom it can die and be saved—every bird and wild flower, every gnat whose wings glint in the sunlight, every grain of dust. We must care for every least part of the earth for "the whole of creation is groaning, awaiting its deliverance." All that we care for and cherish, even the least little things, become part of our fullness of life and remain forever within our own salvation.

We too are looking for a savior into whom we can die and be saved forever, a savior who will put his own spirit on us so that it might return to him bearing us with it. God has involved himself in our history. He has put his Spirit on us. At those times when we were so fragmented, struggling to be faithful, our decisions of state were also his decisions. He has no hidden plan up his sleeve for us to discover. We have received his Spirit. We are more than we appear to be. For that reason he will save us. He is the God of the living, not the God of dead memories or dead people. When we die back into him, the God of life, we are truly saved. It is today we do this. But again, only those who believe can know this. No scientist or theologian can demonstrate it.

What to do

Meditation has to do with:	*Contemplation* has to do with:
ideas	symbols
reasoning	wonder
seeking	intuition
doing	receiving

Both demand concentration. Compare your concentration at prayer with that of famous golfers, baseball players, gymnasts and so on, at their craft.

Find a symbol:
  visual—the cross, mandala, tree, lighted candle . . .
  audible—music, flowing water, traffic, the wind . . .
  active—dance, gesture, clapping hands, quiet walk . . .
Allow the symbol to evoke a response from deep within yourself.

Wonder about your response, what it might mean, in the context of God. What might God be saying to you here and now?

Has Scripture something to say about it? Go with it to God.

Surrender yourself to his Spirit. He pours it out upon you through the medium of the insignificant as well as the significant events of your history, and not just when you are formally at prayer or worship.

11. Work

Aristotle wrote somewhere that "all life is divided into work and play." Anything that is a universal human experience has to have a spirituality and a theology. It has to have a relationship to God in our lives and be a prayer form. Work is an expenditure of energy. Play restores it. Work prolongs the creative impulse of God and leads us to him.

The expenditure of energy itself is not work. To be work the activity must flow from an idea. The idea is impressed on something else, bringing it to a greater perfection. Only humans work. The birds and animals follow a blind instinct. They cannot improvise, improve or correct their labor. They cannot be creative. In fact, very little work is really creative. For that you need the leap of intuition. Most work is dull and reasoned repetition at best, drudgery at worst. It is the creative aspect that dignifies work. Without it work is only labor, no matter how purposeful it may be. Even the birds and beasts have a purpose in what they do.

I spent two years in Rome getting a degree in Canon Law. There was no creativity in it and very little purpose. For the most part it was mind-boggling labor. There is a need for law, not to determine who are right and who are wrong, but to protect the loving from the unloving. It is a better thing to have nothing whatever to do with protectors. Law can be a powerful weapon in the hands of insecure protectors. Law was never meant to be an instrument of power in the Church. The only power the Church is supposed to have is the power to lay down its life for others. At any rate, the idea of somebody in a contemplative life-style getting a degree in Canon Law is hilarious. Canon law is for people who like crossword and jigsaw puzzles. It is also helpful for people who like to keep other people in line. There is an opinion that if Christians would only listen to their Church legislators things would go smoothly. This misses the whole point that salvation is a messy business, not only from the aspects of being saved out of sin rather than out of virtue, but also from the aspect of the unexpected elements in the lives of creative, intuitive people. Canon lawyers do not know what to do with people who are "free with the freedom of the children of God." Biblical or not, the idea is an insult to the whole system.

Working at a degree in Canon Law was a matter of storing up facts. But it was also possible to go back over the examinations given in previous years, intuit certain patterns, and come up with a reasonably close estimate as to what would be asked. I was fortunate enough to be able to make several accurate predictions in this manner and was licensed for my labor. I did learn, however, that law protects freedom. It is not our master. When it fails in its purpose it should be ignored, for the simple reason that society must have changed since its promulgation. Perhaps that discovery alone gave purpose to my two years. Another purposeful factor was the change that took place within myself. When I left the abbey I was a complete fanatic, at least in a few areas. When I returned I was a little more human. I have found out by experience many times since then that when our lives are too narrow, when we are focused on one thing or project only, no matter how valuable it may be, our spirit will always break out in some form of fanaticism or obsession with somebody or something else. Becoming more human and humane is a good work. While in Rome I hung around with James, a monk from Ireland. He seldom came to class; he didn't have to since he had a photographic memory. He maintained that if he never showed up he would never be missed. It was interesting watching that theory being tried out on the Jesuits. Meanwhile he worked hard at getting a suntan out at the beach where I occasionally accompanied him. It was an enjoyable way to cure fanaticism.

There is a time-honored tradition of looking at asceticism as the work aspect of spirituality and mysticism as rest and play. I had been fanatical about the ascetic value of fasting. It was hard work, indeed, and not entirely misplaced, but it had little to do with the fact that monastic literature had always held fasting in high esteem. There is an instinct in all of us, largely dormant, which can be very destructive when undisciplined. We have a drive to transcend the body by asceticism and the mind by mysticism. The reckless exploits of the young are their way of tasting the thrill of transcendence. Disciplined, the drive is not only good but necessary. After all, who wants to be a vegetable? Undisciplined, it is a form of pride in direct opposition to the mystery of the incarnation. Jesus, our only way to the Father, accepted the incomplete human condition and transformed it from within. He did not vanquish it in any guru-like fashion. But we have to arrive at discipline. We are not born with it. Nor is ignorance or innocence any guarantee of discipline. Some of the ancient Celtic and Egyptian monks would, on occasion, spend a night in a brothel to establish the fact to their own satisfaction that they had finally conquered the urge, and had arrived at passionlessness. Or at least, that was the story they told their abbots the following morning. Eventually the practice had to be condemned because the proof was so slow in forthcoming. Being a celibate is hard work if one has to get out there and prove it. On the other hand, as in any other area of growth, if it is not challenged and there are not any demands for discipline, one's innocence is quite likely to be a wishy-washy lack of personality.

"All asceticism and no mysticism makes Jack a dull boy," to give a twist to a proverb. My fasting was excessive. It was painful to sit because of the bones. I had been reading about starving people in India and elsewhere. I felt that praying for them (there was not much else a Trappist could do) without experiencing what they experienced did not make any sense. But there were other elements in it, elements of rebellion and of a death-wish. Our motives are frequently very complex. I'm not proud of this fasting thing, but it was a good learning experience. We know only what we have experienced, and I feel I know something about being deprived of food. The period lasted three years.

One of the more difficult aspects of fasting lay in coping with an altogether irrational sense of pride. The fact that I could face it and deal with it did not mean that it would go away. There was the awareness of being an intelligent spirit-person. The temptation suggested that it was a humiliation, something to be despised, to have to prolong one's life by eating something purely physical that grew out of the earth. It is a very interesting experience to arrive at a point of near starvation where one feels it might be possible to live without eating—to be, as it were, a purely spiritual person. The incongruity of the suggestion, coming as it did from very deep within myself, made the whole thing sort of humorous in a sardonic fashion. The spirit side mocking the physical and vice versa. As a denial of my physical side, that my body was me, it was a denial of myself as well as of the whole spirituality of the incarnation. But it was an experience I could not have had in any other way except, perhaps, through some sort of false mysticism. Another aspect of the temptation lay in the eating itself. The very appearance of containers of food looked crude and vulgar, reminding one of how animal a thing it is to have to eat. Some years later, when I was back to normal, I got an enormous charge out of an experience I had with a friend of mine in San Francisco. He also was a dabbler in asceticism and mysticism. I had invited him to dinner, and not knowing that he was on a vegetarian kick suggested that he order a steak. "Seeing somebody with a steak," he replied, "always reminds me of a dog eating meat."

I learned something else about hungry people. When I woke up at night with cramps in my legs from poor circulation and malnutrition I would have an overpowering urge to go down to the kitchen and steal food. The curious thing was not that I felt hungry. That sensation leaves one very early on in fasting. It was a deep instinctive drive to save life. From then on I could not ever have anything but compassion for the hungry who steal to live. It has nothing to do with malice and is virtually uncontrollable.

Mental energy is another by-product of fasting. This is more of a hindrance than a help for anyone trying to lead a contemplative life. One gets too busy. My capacity for manual work was not diminished although it was a matter of dogged endurance. The endurance came from the mental energy. There was a period in there when my job was to pound in fence posts with a crowbar. Walking to work made my diaphragm flop up and down, causing sharp intakes of breath. Even my prayer was work, fanatical work. I would pray for an hour and a half at a time with outstreched arms, in a sense with an outstreched mind. The flaw in the whole thing lay in knowing that I could do it, that I was good at it. In other words, it was prideful stupidity. And yet, I learned a lot—what fasting does for one's prayer life, sex life (total extinction), and one's work life. I know how it affects one's thinking, and I know how the destitute feel. At the time I had to know, and I am glad I know even though the whole thing was very rash.

The sculptor with his granite and the farmer with his land may produce a work of art. But the great work is the struggle to become a whole person, to live as Jesus lived. The saint is the great workman, and the work of salvation is the great art.

What to do

Do something creative as an expression of your spirit and faith.

You might like to write a haiku—five syllables in the first line, seven in the second and five in the third. Ideally it should be a response of your spirit to something observed in nature, with a reference to one of the seasons. (At the moment I see a robin pulling a worm out of the ground.)

You might like to try something abstract in paint or charcoal and add a caption by way of reflection.

Bring the insight into God's presence. Enter the silence and surrender.

> "The early robin
> kills the springtime early worm . . .
> Lord, may I come late?"

12. Play

Work, even when creative, is an expenditure of energy. The energy must be restored. Give a horse enough oats and sleep, refuel an engine and they will be able and ready to go again. It is not that way with humans. The energy expended is not merely physical. Psychic and spiritual energy must constantly be restored. The warden of a prison knows that the worst punishment he can inflict on an inmate is solitary confinement. Solitary confinement is all right for an animal that has his food and sleep—although he will rarely mate successfully in it. The trouble with humans is that there is nothing to rest the mind in solitary isolation. Reason races on. We need leisure or play to survive as human persons.

Play can be divided roughly into entertainment and recreation. Entertainment comprises all forms of play that have to do with competition, skill, struggle, excitement. Recreation, or more strictly re-creation, has to do with the aesthetic sense, music, art, literature, intuition, contemplation. We have to discover a spirituality of play—play as a form of prayer.

Let us approach a football game with an open mind and try to analyze it. At first sight there are twenty-two men kicking and carrying a bag of wind round a field. There are sixty thousand fans in a state of near frenzy cheering them on for doing it. We are told that the object of the game is to get the ball across the end line. As totally dispassionate onlookers it strikes us that we have a great waste of energy here. Why not, in a peace-loving manner, call a truce, march down and place the ball in the desired position? However logical and adult this decision might be, it is not acceptable to the fans. On the other hand, judging by the guaranteed salaries and immobile expressions, it would seem very acceptable to the players. The problem is that it would end the play. We realize now that the play is in the struggle. Half of the players are pitted against the other half. If the struggle is diminished because the game is too onesided the fans get bored. They need the excitement. Even a broken leg would add a great deal to the thrill situation. Without the excitement, everybody feels cheated. The struggle reaches a high of excitement in tension situations, such as when the ball is on the one-yard line. This is what the fans came to see, the very core of the game. Our next insight is that to enter into the spirit of the thing we must choose sides. Having chosen a side, with the firm desire that it should be the victor, we discover that in some sense our side is the "good" side. It is threatened by the visitors, which makes the visitor "evil" or "bad" in some manner. With tension built up as the ball is on the one-yard line we scream for a resolution of the situation. With the resolution tension is released and the fans explode in approval. We either lose their advantage or we save the situation. Now we are beginning to understand something. It is really, though symbolically, a struggle between good and evil, between being saved and being lost. "He saved the day" or "we lost" we say. The fans are projecting out on to the field the struggle between good and evil that is in their own hearts. They are cheering the victory of good over evil. The tension between good and evil is a universal experience. Entertainment is necessary to defuse it.

When the first European settlers came to America they were surprised, and a little shocked, to find the native population playing gambling games and wondered who had taught them. The first time I played roulette in a casino at Lake Tahoe I won sixteen dollars. When my money was on the red I found red to be very good and black very evil. For most people gambling is not a matter of greed or the desire to get something for nothing. Most thinking people go to a casino quite prepared to lose a few dollars for the sake of the play. And the play consists in beating the system which is favored against them—outwitting and defeating the evil. The struggle, the tension and the resultant exhiliration when the bell rings for a jackpot are well worth the inevitable outcome.

This same form of struggle is also the basis for many other types of entertainment—the good guys versus the bad guys on television and in novels are an example. The good guys always win. They have to win or the show would be out of harmony with our desire for the good to triumph. The challenge is also there in racing cars, horse races, track meets and pinball machines. People climb Mount Everest "because it is there" as the first man to reach the top put it. We have an urge to transcend our environment, ourselves really. We have to overcome the law of entropy in our behavior and in nature. It is a saved-and-lost situation, and every fan is looking for a messiah.

The saved-and-lost situation has very frightening aspects when military men are tempted to play the game of war. It is the ultimate struggle. And it is fascinating because it is entertaining. If anybody has any doubts about that he should read the autobiographies of the military leaders of Word War II. They reveal an excessive preoccupation with the game of outwitting the enemy, with glory in great battles. There are instances of a viewpoint such as one might have in a chess game—how many men could be sacrificed to gain an objective and how many tanks. There is considerable peevishness with the amount of press coverage the leader is getting back home. And one of them admitted to a sense of letdown when peace was declared because "there would be no more glory." And yet, even the horrors of war reflect our desires that the good should triumph, at least the apparent good. We hunger for salvation.

The victory on the playing field, or on the battlefield, is only partial and provisional. It is a symbolic gesture more than an accomplishment. As such it must be played over and over again. As long as the struggle continues in our hearts we shall be fascinated and entertained by tension situations. We might ask if there is any end to the struggle. Is there some event or some place where evil in all its naked power clashed with the totality of good, and what was the outcome? The answer, of course, lies in the death and resurrection of Christ. Evil was defeated and good resurrected into unending life while soldiers gambled at the foot of the cross. Now we know what entertainment is all about. The sixty thousand fans are cheering on Christ on the cross, although they do not know it. He triumphed

65

in a curious way. He lost but he accepted his loss and this made him the greater person . . . "forgive them, Father." Those who love unselfishly always win whether they triumph or are defeated. Games are a form of prayer for those who have contemplative insight.

Recreation differs from entertainment. People need to relax. They say, "I need to be left alone. I want to get away from it all." But when left alone they find themselves restless, the mind and imagination racing. What they need is beauty. Beauty is to the mind what food and drink are to the body. Beauty sets reasoning at rest. We do not reason about beauty. We drink it in intuitively. It is not the end result of a process of logic. Let us take as an example our reaction to a beautiful sunset. There is no discussion—so much blue over there, so much red and purple here. We gaze on the sunset with wonder, contemplating it with a growing inner silence. The result is a sense of restfulness, a sense of being lifted up above the petty things of everyday living. We begin to say, "I wonder why we have to be so petty, so competitive, so defensive?" The mind is rested. We feel strong again, at peace, able to face another week, able to live with a less than ideal situation. People do this sort of thing all the time without reflection. Society has to have its measure of contemplation or contemplatives to keep it from going mad. We need all the beauty we can get. It re-creates us. Contemplation is rest.

The businessman goes out to play a game of golf, not to struggle or be competitive and win but to enjoy the green earth, to enjoy companionship. The city sets aside its most valuable property to make a park because people need beauty. People in slums grow flowers in window boxes because they realize intuitively that it helps them stay human. They know from experience that there is most crime where there is least beauty. No matter how practical or pragmatic people might be they always seem to find beauty. Without it we become hard and unfeeling from the stress of coping, advancing and defending ourselves. More than others, politicians, priests and the Joint Chiefs of Staff need beauty to combat the destructive force of power. Business executives need it to counteract the corruption of wealth. The punishment of solitary confinement is the escalation of inner anguish that is not relieved by beauty. The more sensitive and creative the person the more painful the confinement. Beauty is the common basis of all the fruits of the spirit: music, art, poetry, love and quiet prayer.

Greater than the beauty of the sunset is the beauty of people's moral acts. An act of genuine unselfishness can bring tears to the eyes of the beholder. Tears are a reaction to an intuitive grasp of beauty. Portia, in *The Merchant of Venice:* "I am always sad when I hear sweet music." Tears are a way of saying that our inmost depths have been opened up. At our deepest level we have a hunger for an absolute beauty. The tears are the surfacing of that hunger, the ache for a perfection that eludes us, the sense of exile from a paradise lost or from one yet to be found. Beauty is the key that unlocks our deepest spirit. For that reason, stories of heroism are always newsworthy. People hunger for a glimpse of their better self revealed in the actions of others. The reaction to the beauty in an heroic act is not logical but intuitive—wondering, understanding. We grasp what it means and share it, becoming what we contemplate—"Next time," we tell ourselves, "I will be able to do that." We feel instinctively that this act of generous love expresses precisely what our deepest commitment to life is all about—even if at the moment imitation is beyond us. People who have no form of organized religion whatever honor the saints because of the beauty of their heroic love. Beauty reveals our immeasurable longing for fulfillment and in some respects leads us into it.

Monastic liturgy has an austere beauty all its own when it is done with care. It is not given to emotionalism. It cannot be. It touches deeper levels. But austere beauty as a steady diet has its limitations. It was good liturgy to break the routine, saddle up a few horses and go up through the sage to the top of the Wasatch foothills. There in workshirt and jeans we celebrated the Eucharist with the same spirit as Moses on Sinai and Jesus on the mount of Transfiguration. Liturgy can be a beautiful and overwhelming encounter with God when it is liberated from the grasp of rubricians.

Beauty can be defined as "the splendor of form shining on proportioned parts of matter." The definition is not altogether satisfactory. Young people, who have not yet made their faces, are oftentimes quite pretty. Elderly people with kind and wrinkled faces are beautiful. It is a splendor or effulgence of the spirit shining from within. The splendor is what is intuitively grasped. Something like this is said of the humanity of Jesus: ". . . he is the radiant light of God's glory" (Heb 1:3); ". . . God's glory, shining on the face of Christ" (II Cor 4:6); ". . . and we saw his glory, the glory that is his as the only Son of the Father, full of grace and truth" (Jn 1:14).

Christ's humanity reveals, and at the same time for our sake, tempers, the absolute beauty of the Father. In our contemplative moments we can gaze on that beauty. Our hunger for beauty is our hunger for Christ. The glory of God, expressed humanly in Christ, is the only adequate rest for weary minds. It lifts us above the petty refusal to love, re-creates us, enabling us to live fully human lives. It is the world's peace. "If we live our lives in the light, as he is in the light, we are in union with one another" (I Jn 1:6, 7). "All of us, then, reflect the glory of the Lord with uncovered faces; the same glory, coming from the Lord who is spirit, transforms us into his very likeness, in an ever greater degree of glory" (II Cor 3:18). This is a description of contemplative praying. Musing and wondering about the beauty of God revealed in Christ, we are transformed into his likeness. We become of one mind with him. And our growth into his likeness is as unlimited and as unending as is the ever greater God.

Finally, there is the beatific vision, eternal rest—not the end but the fullness of life. It is the clear unmediated vision of God in all his splendor, immediate awareness of God and of all things else in Him. All who love beauty are loving this Absolute Beauty. Every child who picks a wild flower, everyone who sits by the sea or walks in a park is professing faith in God's beauty. They are hungering for absolute rest, for the new creation that he alone can give. And he knows that about them, and credits it to them, whether they are aware of it or not. In contemplative praying we go directly through the beauty of little things to touch the beauty of God. The business executive on the golf course, the woman watering flowers in the slum, the campers, trailer homes, beaches are all faith in beatific vision. They are a contemplative prayer form.

What to do

Look for the beauty and you will find it.

Everything has a beautiful aspect—the color, light, shape.

Look again at people and try to see beneath the mask. See them in the context of their whole lives and not as isolated in this moment.

Sit with God by a stream, or in the woods, or listening to the city noises. Let your awareness be expanded. "Be still and see how good the Lord is."

Listen to music and wonder what the music might be saying to God. Let the music do the speaking.

Let the beauty bring rest to the mind. Let it strengthen and expand your spirit beyond the petty.

Let the mind go quietly to God and give yourself to him.

13. The Mystics

In spite of our sinfulness and neglect we constantly experience ourselves as called by God. Time and again we are aware that he has
called us into the environment of his personal presence, challenging
us, giving himself to us in goodness and love. However, since his self-
gift is not imposed, this call and presence, for all that we cannot ignore it, may be translated by our conscious mind as darkness, silence
or even an apparent absence of God. He is experienced as the ultimate meaning of our lives, the real truth of our existence. God's gift
of himself is made freely, as an invitation, that we might respond
freely. What matters is our response. The form the response might
take is of no great consequence. Mysticism is the experimental
awareness, provisional and tentative, of his presence as gift and of
our response to it. It is, therefore, a dialogue with God, not a vision
of the essence of the divinity. "No man can see God and live." It is
an awareness of his presence in one's spirit, in darkness or light, pain
or joy, where he offers and reveals himself. This awareness and its re-
sulting dialogue flow from love and are the mystics' highest activity.
God is known in this dialogue of love in a manner beyond all images
and symbols, beyond abstract or discursive thought, in a union of
spirit with Spirit. It is a contact of the spirit and whole being of the
mystic with transcendental reality, with the fullness of being as such
with the ground and source of all that is.

We must take a glance, however superficial it may be, at what the mystics tell us about some aspects of their prayer. They tell us that their contact with God takes place in the ground, or apex, or center of the soul. We would say it takes place in "the core of the personality," in the depths of the spirit where we experience an opening on the infinite. It was in those depths that they received in gift what they could never attain to by their own powers, a union of love with God in an overwhelming joy. The result was an expansion and perfection of their personalities, a confirmation in their own essential freedom. They would no longer be dependent on created things for an identity, but dependent on God.

Some stressed growth into the "image and likeness" of God. The possibility of transformation was there to begin with. Following this path, Bernard of Clairvaux and William of St. Thierry maintained that the image always remained but the likeness had to be recovered. Transformed by humility into the likeness of God by meditation on the passion of Christ, the person of prayer travels from the "region of unlikeness" to the "region of likeness." The soul becomes "the mirror of love" in which God is reflected. They stressed the knowledge that came from love. God is not seen in himself but as reflected in the transformed person. For Ruysbroeck, Gerhard Groote and Gerlach Peeters, the mystics of the Low Countries, a person is transformed by his or her relationship to Christ. "One must be like him in his humanity before sharing in his divinity." The mystic, they tell us, is the perfectly balanced person who comes from God in love and returns to him through works of active love for others. The German mystics Tauler, Eckhart and Suso stress the divinization of the human person by sharing in the uncreated life of God. The quickest way is through compassion for the suffering humanity of Jesus. The mystic is a lover who identifies with Jesus, who is love. That love was revealed in its most demanding form on the cross. The face of Christ crucified is the face of ultimate reality, the pathway to deliverance.

The English mystics flourished in the fourteenth century. Their most profound written work is *The Cloud of Unknowing.* According to it, a new stage of prayer takes over when images and discursive thought have been left behind. It is "a naked concentration on God, a thick cloud of forgetting." One remains silent and unknowing before God, not seeking anything, although God may at times pierce the cloud to reveal his secret mystery. Walter Hilton (d. 1396) writes of the need to break down the image of sin by meditation on the Passion. One goes through a period of great joy, he tells us, but then there is inevitably a period of darkness and purification, the necessary cleansing of our subliminal self-centered depths. Julian of Norwich, an anchoress of that city, is the most delightful and the most readable of the English mystics. Her "shewings" are full of a theological optimism, of tender love and a refreshing approach to God: "All thing shall be well, and all thing shall be well, and all manner of thing shall be well." Devotion to the humanity of Christ was also stressed by Teresa of Avila and other Spanish mystics. Teresa writes of the direction she got from the Jesuit, Diego de Cetina:

> He told me to take a scene from the Passion for my prayer every day . . . where I would think only of the humanity . . . a greater knowledge began to take hold of my soul . . . I began to have a new love of the Sacred Humanity. Prayer began to appear as a building already well founded.

St. John of the Cross tells us that things can have an authentic value only for the person of prayer. A change in a person always reveals a change in his appreciation of things. He tells us that faith is a fathomless reality revealing God's hiddenness. Its primary image is the passion of Christ, which is love within an immeasurable faith. For John, another image of faith was the nothingness at the heart of all created things.

The mystics seemed to be of an "all or nothing" temperament, capable of a passionate love. We have witness of this capacity for love in Augustine, Francis of Assisi, Angelo of Foligno, Catherine of Siena and others as they struggled with their sexuality and their love. There are no born mystics. Their prayer was a long struggle upwards. Although, in their way of expressing themselves, they seemed at times to bypass the world, they never made the mistake of rejecting it. They were poets, they loved music and nature and people. They rejected all aggressiveness, boasting and greed. Frugality, mercy and staying out of the center of the stage were their characteristics. They had a capacity for intuition, an appreciation of beauty and a capacity for pleasure which was required for the mystical experience. They had joy and a sense of humor. It was these characteristics that marked them off from fanatics and protected and preserved the authenticity of their prayer experience. They knew that there were no limits set on loving and that, therefore, their prayer was always only a beginning. It was not possible to be vain about it. They also knew that it was only by love that the world could be transformed. They challenge us to follow in their footsteps, howsoever poorly we might be able to do so.

What to do

Be silent, recollected in body and spirit.

"Do not imitate but interiorize Christ." (The Fathers)

Joy is complete in the possession of the total good. Christ within you is All. You have arrived. "That is all."

"Eternal life is knowing you" (Jn 17:3).

Be a person-in-awe-of-God.

Be simple, no pros and cons.

Be unhistorical in the eternal "now."

Surrender and praise.

"The labor of a lifetime is crowned in contemplation" (Josef Pieper).

14. "Out of the Body"

The purpose of prayer is a union of love with God—the beginning of prayer being wonder, the end being surrender. However, along the way we may have certain experiences that have a formative or educative value. They do not, unfortunately, guarantee that we are loving people. They are not the end at which one aims, nor does recalling them recreate their moment of grace. They might best be forgotten. But one reason only—that an experience from which we have not learned anything is a waste of time—may permit us to recall and analyze them. The Apostles recalled the mount of Transfiguration, but Jesus' question was not whether or not they had had an experience, but whether or not they could drink from the chalice from which he drank.

One such experience is what is called "out of the body." This may take place as a result of a certain set of circumstances—physical, psychological and spiritual. It may be an explosive reaction to some form of confinement, but that does not take from it the unique reality it is to the artist or to the person of prayer. It is a moment of intuition and understanding, of connaturality and union. It is an experience of what a fullness of life and joy can be. One does not, of course, leave the body; it seems that way because what is experienced is some sort of immediate intuitive awareness of one's spirit and its relationship to all that is other than itself. The substance of this experience is active within all of us, but it remains below consciousness

74

for the most part. When it surfaces, people describe it in words and symbols distinctively their own. Reflection is impossible unless the experience is translated into symbols, concepts and words. Much is lost, or even distorted, in the translation. Words fail, with the result that one is reduced to saying: "It seemed as if . . ." The experience will not only be translated differently by different people, it will also be translated differently by the same person should it be repeated.

With all of those provisos it is only with a great deal of hesitation that I describe two such experiences, one more or less in the language of "being," the other more in the language of "doing." The occasion of the first was in the morning at a moment of deep recollection. Imagination and emotions were totally at rest. Some sort of rhythm of life in the body slowed down. It was not just the heartbeat, but something more pervasive like life itself. As it slowed down another rhythm of life in the spirit seemed to emerge and grow. I cannot say what it was. For a moment I wondered if this were death. There was no fear at all because emotions and imaginings were stilled. I wondered, but without any great curiosity if what would be left would be a corpse or an idiot. The thought quickly vanished as I began to experience a very pleasant sense of weightlessness and freedom. All confinement seemed to disappear as I felt as if I were coming out of my body and hovering over it. Everything seemed translucent—full of a soft light like the dawn. The body and, in fact, all individual things were soon forgotten and I felt open to the whole of reality. I had no form or shape. I faced in all directions, because there really was no direction. I was becoming fully alive. I began to realize a presence that was everywhere. All "wheres" seemed to be present to me. As a consequence, there was stillness, no motion either in the sense of local motion or achievement. This was so because, without leaving where I was I seemed to be present to all the extensions of being. I seemed one with being. I could savor or relish, in complete bliss, the reality of "being" itself, and the reality of my own being and existing. I began to experience what might be called a complete integration of my being. My oneness was not that of an object that could be shattered or divided, but the complete simplicity and indivisibility of spiritual being. This extension of my spirit to the whole of reality caused a wild, mad joy within me, compared with which the greatest joy in the body was as nothing. Life was never really experienced until this moment.

At this point I became aware of a sort of borderline. I felt that if

I crossed that line life in the body would cease altogether. I felt also that crossing it would have to be a willful act on my part, but one, were I close enough to the line, I could not resist. The desire for total fulfillment and total joy would be too intense. Crossing over would mean a surrender to total life in the Spirit. To do so would be final. There would be no coming back since to return would imply something wanting in the fullness, something yet to be achieved, some want of rest and stillness. I remained there for a short time, full of light, energy and amazed joy. Then the rhythm of life in the body picked up and I returned to find that what we call living is really only an illusion of life. We live hallucinated by multiplicity. Life, as we experience it, seems no more than a spark thrown off from the struggle between the desire of the body and the desire of the spirit. It is not the full flame of union.

However, although life as we experience it daily seemed opaque compared with this "out of the body" experience, individual things had subsequently taken on a whole new meaning. I saw them charged with importance because they had "being." They existed. They were. Each in its own way partook in and reflected the fullness of being. Every day for months I sang aloud in my off-key fashion and praised God simply because things were. No matter how unimportant or insignificant they were in themselves—the wild flowers, the sage, the wind, the smell of the earth—I was full of joy for them. After three months the feeling gradually tapered off, but nothing is insignificant anymore. One might ask if there was anything of God in this whole experience. My reaction of joy and praise to God for being would seem to imply that yes, there was much of God in it. But there was no objectified, "out there" sense of God. When one is surrounded by a symphony of live music, when the music is pounding and pulsating in one's ears and heart, thrilling every nerve-ending, are we present to the musicians? Does the question even have any meaning? All I know is that every atom of being is exploding with the life and presence of God.

The experience was repeated once more during prayer. I had been making a conscious effort to focus attention and concentrate. After a little while all individual things, concepts, symbols, fantasies began to leave my mind of themselves. Unlike on other occasions I did not seem to have to drop them. They began to go out like soap bubbles popping. I was moving away without effort from individual things to the universal, from categories of time and space to transcendent openness. It was like coming out of a cave into the light. The distance seemed very great but there was deep rest and stillness. So it appeared as if I were being carried rapidly, but in exhilerating slow motion and great smooth leaps, out into space. "Things" departed and I seemed face to face with a boundless, imageless God. This God could not be contained in any word, G-O-D, symbol or concept. I remained there in a sort of gagged, speechless wonder. Without observing them I felt filled with compassion for all created things, they being so fragile in the light of God's greatness. There was love and compassion for everything and everybody.

Several things happend here. There was a clear sense of the loss of "self," the empirical self of everyday consideration. There was no question of being in some sort of trance, nor was it a matter of not adverting to myself. There was a clear consciousness of my individual, personal existence, yet when I turned to reflect on myself there was nothing there to see or observe. There was only God within and without, God boundless and absolute, the fullness of God everywhere. Afterward, I recalled a passage in the *Dialogues* of St. Catherine of Genoa where she writes:

> I will have nothing to do with a love that would be for God or in God. I cannot bear the word "for" or "in," because they denote something that may be in between me and God. My me is God. It is the same when I speak of being. My being is God, not by participation but by true transformation of my own being (Dialogues XIV).

St. Bernard writes in *Sermon 31 on the Canticle:*

> May my soul depart from remembrance of this present, put away, not desire for but even images of material things, and have union with what is pure spirit. This going forth is alone, or principally, what is called contemplation.

He tells us that this union is possible because of God's absolute spirituality, and the spirituality of our own person. It is not a fusion but a union of wills in love.

For it is the word not speaking but entering, not loquacious but efficacious, not in any form but formative (Sermon 31).

and:

How can God be All in all, if anything of man remains in man?
The substance indeed will remain but in another form, another glory (Sermon 71).

He tells us that reason sleeps but love remains watchful. "Love-which-is-understanding" was for Bernard a way of knowing God that transcended reason.

Another aspect of the experience was this: though the awareness of God prevented the mind from focusing on any individual thing, it did not make me unaware of reality. In fact, it heightened the sense of reality. The whole world, in contrast to the immensity of God, seemed to shrink down to where it was manageable or understandable. There was a sense of the whole of created reality and it was small compared with God. Later I recalled a saying of Julian of Norwich about seeing the whole world and it seemed no bigger than a hazelnut in God's hand. St. Gregory writes of an experience of St. Benedict in which, standing at the window of his abbey, he saw the whole world in a ray of light. This view of the world made it look like a map on which I saw that everybody had to plot a journey to God. The world was merely a reference point. What mattered was not the point of reference but the destination. All, rich and poor alike, the powerful and the exploited, have to make this journey. In the light of this understanding, things that seemed important were now seen in a new perspective, their importance only being relative. This did not contradict the importance of matters such as human and civil rights, justice and the right of each individual to a way of life worthy of the dignity of being human. It complemented these important matters by stressing that they are vital in view of life's destination. The end of the human family determines the form our living should take. This "out of the body" experience does not justify a want of concern for others. It demands concern.

This experience is not the end of the search for God. In a way it is only the beginning. It is a translation into experience of what is daily happening at the depth of our spirit where God is transforming

78

us into his likeness. This transformation is happening, not only when we are at formal prayer, but whenever we are going beyond ourselves in caring, loving and sharing with others. The experience itself is only a glimpse in the mirror of our spirit when it is not clouded over. But a glimpse in a mirror does not necessarily improve our eyesight.

Spirit remains a mystery to us. We have no faculty to analyze it directly. This may leave us confused at times as to whether we are praying or not, whether we have a spiritual life or not. Is anything happening? Is it worth the effort to continue taking time for prayer? Messages and insights are not what matter. We have to sit with God somewhat in the manner we might sit with our health, a sort of non-experience, or an experience of harmony rather than of insights. We have to persevere facing a blank wall. There will be luminous moments. They are few and we may not lust after them. What we need is a dedicated willingness.

What to do

Nothing creative comes out of routine, only more of the same. Break routine.

There is no way out of the desert. All the horizons look alike. Going north you meet yourself coming south, going east you meet yourself coming west. To escape the desert you must transcend it with your spirit like circles in a pond.

Do not try to experience God at the expense of your humanity. He is God in this present reality, this moment, this place, this feeling.

See him coming out of the tomb
    in the smile of a child,
    in a wild flower or a wild person,
    in neon lights and highway signs,
    in green grass and fields of grain.
Hear him
    in the roar of traffic,
    in the sound of absolute silence,
    in the wind and rain.
Love him
    in love and neglect,
    in pain and indifference,
    in enemies and friends.

15. Friendship

What begins in a search through nothingness for God and for meaning ends in friendship. In our surrender to God we come to know him as friend: "I shall not call you servants anymore ... I call you friends" (Jn 15:15). We not only have a hunger for friendship, we have a basic need for it. It is one of life's necessities. Without love, a child will die in the cradle and an old man will die in a retirement home. Without friendships something is dead within us. A healthy openness, frankness and sincerity, as well as an attitude of respect are fundamental as a foundation for prayer. These qualities are developed in friendships. Friendship does not manipulate or cling. It demands that people be open to reality and support one another. It brings with it an empathetic knowledge of the other, an understanding that comes from love and compassion. It is the opposite of infatuation which is a denial of one's personality and a form of slavery. Friendships happen. They cannot be commanded or earned.

Friends grow together. They are not friends if they connive in each other's mediocrity. Friends challenge each other. Friendship is joy-filling but also humbling. Writers on the spiritual life have not always taken it as seriously as it demands. But the Celtic monks encouraged everybody to have an *anam-chara,* a soul-friend who would direct and support the monk in his spiritual journey. Later on, other Benedictine and Cistercian monks studied Cicero's *De Amicitia.* Aelred, Abbot of Rievaulx, wrote a short book on friendship that came out of his discussions with a small group of his monks. "Friendship with anybody is ultimately friendship with Christ," he wrote. Much of the creative output of the great people of prayer was the direct result of their friendships. There were Jerome and Paula, Francis of Assisi and the Countess. On his deathbed Francis asked that a message be sent to Rome to the Countess asking her to come and bring some of her honey-cakes which he so liked. She came. There is a simplicity in the life of a whole person that can express heroic charity in commonplace things. The Countess came. Christ would have come. There were Blessed Jordan of Saxony and Blessed Diana, both Dominicans. She saved his letters in which he mentions his distress at her tears as they parted. The saints were disciplined people but they were anything but cold and stoical. Whole people are sensitive people. Others who influenced each other in creative ways were John of the Cross and Teresa of Avila. The reform of the Carmelite Order owed much to their friendship. Francis de Sales and Jane de Chantal, Vincent de Paul and Louise de Marillac were founders of religious congregations. Alone they could not have done it. The key to their friendship was their mutual love of Christ. It enabled them to transcend the purely physical. Unselfish friendships have changed the face of the earth. Indulgent relationships have marred it. Friends have the power to draw the best out of us. They may one day enable us to transcend ourselves heroically. For the moment, however, it is sufficient that they call us out of our isolation and enable us to celebrate living.

To have formed a few very deep friendships is the blessing of a lifetime. The trouble is that people capable of deep friendships are usually very creative and dynamic, which inevitably means that they will be scattered abroad doing something worthwhile. One keeps contact, by mail, by an occasional visit. But the result is always the same, a deep sense of peace and strength, a knowledge that one is loved and accepted for oneself, a "salvation" experience. Jesus gave his special friendship to Peter, James and the disciple "whom the Lord loved," John. Martha, Mary and Lazarus were also special to him. It is Jesus who is seeking us. If we take the attitude that it is we who are doing the searching we are bound to experience disappointment. Our search is only a response to the fact that he has already touched us. Our response to his "choked-up compassionate love" will be total the day we understand how total is his love for us. Instead of our self-conscious efforts to be "good" we should allow ourselves the luxury of being loved by God. And much of his love for us will be expressed through the medium of our friends' love for us. How else could he reveal it in a way that is tangible? But he will also speak to us within our self-understanding, love us within our self-acceptance, celebrate with us when we celebrate with our friends. "You are my friends, if you do what I command you. . . . What I command you is to love one another" (Jn 15:14, 17). Friends I have in plenty, at the abbey and here at the priory of St. Gertrude where I am chaplain. They give me God and life and love.

What to do

Trust the failing effort in your prayer. God is within it.

For now it is sufficient. Let it purify you of all fear, guilt, frustration, prudery, phoniness and fanaticism.

Have no expectation when entering prayer, no predetermined something that should happen to prove it is worthwhile. Nothing needs to be proved. The time is God's time. Let it be.

Drop all forms of spiritual grasping, all self-pity, all self-importance.

If "nothing" is happening allow it to teach you inner silence, contentment, serenity, understanding, empathy, friendliness and concern.

Celebrate life.

We are always only beginning.